Adobe® Photoshop® Maste

MAGGIE TAYLOR's
LANDSCAPE OF DREAMS

AMY STANDEN

Adobe Photoshop Master Class: Maggie Taylor's Landscape of Dreams

Amy Standen

This Adobe Press book is published by Peachpit
For information on Adobe Press books, contact:
Peachpit
1249 Eighth Street, Berkeley, CA 94710
510/524-2178, 800/283-9444, 510/524-2221 (fax)

To report errors, please send a note to errata@peachpit.com
Peachpit is a division of Pearson Education
For the latest on Adobe Press books, go to www.adobepress.com
Copyright © 2005 by Amy Standen

Editor: Douglas Cruickshank
Senior Executive Editor: Marjorie Baer
Production Editor: Connie Jeung-Mills
Compositor: Kim Scott
Indexer: Karin Arrigoni
Cover and Interior Design: Charlene Charles-Will

ISBN 0-321-30614-7

9 8 7 6 5 4 3 2 1

Printed and bound in the United States of America

For Chris, with love.
— Amy Standen

For Jerry, with love and gratitude for his inspiration.
— Maggie Taylor

(GIRL WITH A BEE DRESS, DETAIL)

Contents

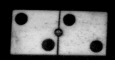

Taylor is too subtle an artist to use these objects as anything more than

clues that we are invited to pursue.

Take her up on it, and you may find that a thread appears.

As you pull it, the mystery unravels.

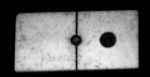

CHAPTER ONE

Memory and Daydream

A YOUNG BALLERINA HALF SMILES at the camera, hands on her hips. She wears what could pass as a 1940s gym outfit for 10-year-old girls: a short-sleeved blouse, bloomers, and thick woolen tights that wrinkle over her knees. Her smile is enigmatic, her expression preternaturally composed for a girl that age. She wears pink ballet slippers, a Zorro mask, and two large yellow antennae from a Luna moth that stick up from her brow like rabbit ears. Nine yellow moths are tied to her waist with blue string; they're either dancing around the girl or trying to get away from her, depending on how you look at it. One moth has broken free; the discarded blue string lies at the girl's feet. Away from the others, it has lost its color and looks ghostly flying off into the night.

The edge of what could be a fruit orchard marks the horizon, bordered at each end by larger trees. The setting is rural, and though there's no obvious menace, darkness seeps in from the edges. It's a vaguely creepy scene, something a child might see looking out into the night from a bedroom window. Like the fear of darkness itself, the threat is suggestive rather than specified; we feel the boogeyman, we don't see him. As in many of Maggie Taylor's

{ Moth dancer, 2004. }

{ Boy who loves water, 2004. }

images, there's something odd about the light in this picture, offsetting the subject from the background. The girl looks lit by the sun, bright and overhead, but it's clearly twilight in the distance, and the crescent, fairy-tale moon has been up for a while. The box she stands on appears to rest on the grassy field, but the girl is more superimposed on her environment than a part of it. Armed with all her fantastical accouterments—moths, antennae, mask—the moth dancer rises out of her gloomy setting with confidence in her gaze. Is this the pose of a girl in triumph over some childhood nightmare?

I looked at this image countless times and appreciated it in many different ways before the story of it finally came to me. This is how Taylor's images often work: what strikes you first is the lushness of them, the color, the expressions on the characters' faces, the odd light, and the composition, all hinting at some buried narrative. Next, one might wonder what the various objects represent; Taylor describes them as "obviously symbolic but not symbolically obvious." Whether it's the moths in *Moth dancer*, the bird and egg in *One and a half sisters*, or the wings of *Maybe never*, Taylor is too subtle an artist to use these objects as anything more than clues that we are invited to pursue. The open stare of the moth dancer is yet another invitation. Take her up on it, and you may find that a thread appears. As you pull it, the mystery unravels.

Often in Taylor's work, that thread tugs at childhood memories and impressions: the fear of the dark (*Moth dancer*); the sensation of being out of place (*Boy who loves water*); deflated expectations (*Party girl*); or sibling relationships (*One and a half*

sisters). That these are, to some extent, universal experiences accounts for part of the power of Taylor's work. Some images yank us back to a distant childhood memory, others to a half-remembered dream; still others articulate an emotion from recent life.

But Taylor's images, while speaking to universal themes, are fundamentally autobiographical. "I believe in making work from my personal experience," she told critic Paul Karabinis in a 1998 interview, "from my own memories and dreams—from my psyche." *Birthday girl*, for example, recalls an ill-fated Taylor family birthday party, an argument, and a cake used in a decidedly un-festive manner. This isn't to suggest that all of Taylor's images can be decoded into a specific incident from her past; few, in fact, are so straightforward. But there's a trace of Taylor in all of these images, which makes an introduction to the artist herself a good place to start.

Maggie Taylor was born in 1961 in Cleveland, Ohio, to James and Sara Taylor, a stockbroker and his wife. Taylor's sister, also named Sara, was three years younger to the day. The Taylors had lived in Ohio for generations, "nice Ohio families, traditional values," as Taylor describes them. The girls took diving lessons and competed in synchronized swimming meets. In the winter, they went tobogganing at the local country club.

Though Taylor was born in Ohio, she considers Florida her native state. In 1972, when she was 11, the family moved to St. Petersburg, where her father had found a job selling municipal bonds. The Florida lifestyle suited them better than Cleveland's.

{ Birthday girl, 2000. }

They lived on Boca Ciega Bay, kept several sailboats, and the family learned to sail, water ski, and fish. Often Taylor would take one of the small sailboats out on the bay, looking for shells and fish in the mudflats.

Apart from genetics, Maggie and Sara had little in common. Sara easily made friends in the neighborhood. "She knew how to talk to anyone, from a grandparent to a stranger we met on vacation," says Taylor. Maggie was an introvert. She spent most of her time in her room. "I was happy being alone. I liked to be in my room alone, to read a book or watch TV alone. Sara was more social. I liked going to the library and getting science fiction books. I was always excited to see the summer reading lists."

Taylor enjoyed school and excelled at it, but bookish isn't the word for her. As a child, she says, "I watched a ton of TV. Way more than normal. Like on a weekend, maybe eight hours a day." Listening to Taylor catalogue her favorite childhood TV shows is like flipping through the pages of a 1970s *TV Guide*: "I watched *Star Trek*, *The Brady Bunch*, *The Partridge Family*, *The Waltons*, *The Mary Tyler Moore Show*, *Bob Newhart*… What else? Oh, *Hawaii Five-O*, *Bewitched*…"

Taylor was, and still is, a glutton for narrative, for gossip, and for all kinds of storytelling, high and low. As a youngster, *Star Trek* and *American Bandstand* filled her weekends. Later, she'd develop an addiction to the daytime soaps. Nowadays, though still an ardent *All My Children* fan, Taylor can speak authoritatively on any game show or reality TV program television has to offer. Not surprisingly, television plays a significant role in Taylor's artistic impulses, her interests, and her aesthetic. Taylor often refers to the people in her images as "characters," particularly those she reuses, such as the downcast, fob-wearing man in *Burn*, a recurring figure in Taylor's work. The implied drama and suspense of many Taylor images is reminiscent of the twists and turns of soap-opera plots (for instance, the mid-flight cake in *Birthday Girl* or the flaming photograph in *Burn*). Even the composition of many Taylor images—a head and chest against a horizontal line—is one she traces to the "talking heads" convention of TV news broadcasts. Television is never

Untitled, 1981.
Untitled, 1982.

the subject of Taylor's work, but, like so many of her other childhood hobbies and interests, it finds other ways into her work.

As much as Taylor loved television, it was not enough of a diversion to keep her home for long. At 12, she began spending summers at camp. At 14, she enrolled in a boarding school. The inveterate urge for independence was setting in. "From the moment I arrived in boarding school, I was thrilled. I was never homesick. I was like 'Where's my mailbox? Where's my room? Let's decorate the room!' I still wasn't very social; I only had a few friends, but I liked the whole scene. I liked being on my own."

In 1979, Taylor began college at Yale and graduated four years later with a degree in philosophy. It was there she discovered that she loved to make art, especially photographs. "Sometime in my sophomore year I got interested in photography and borrowed a camera from my dad, and asked someone to show me how to use the darkroom." Photography, like so many of her childhood hobbies, was a project Taylor could work on alone. The hours spent in a darkroom suited her, as did photography classes, which left her free to improvise and experiment on her own.

As Taylor recalls it, the aesthetic of the Yale photography program in the 1980s was set primarily by the work of documentary photographers of American life like Walker Evans, Lee Friedlander,

Left, *Forget-me-not.*
Below, *Don't pester me.*

and Garry Winogrand. The style was cool, witty, detached, and limited in two significant ways: first, subjects were never staged; second, photographs were always black and white. "Undergraduates were not allowed to work in color," Taylor says, "and of course there were no computers, even our typewriters were barely electric. I had an IBM that was electric but had no memory functions. All papers had to be typed with Wite-Out at the ready. [Experimentation] was encouraged, as long as it was within the narrow parameters of what they considered photography." Most of Taylor's classmates were photographing people, Friedlander-style, but the prospect of approaching strangers intimidated Taylor, so she focused instead on the spaces people leave behind. Wandering through New Haven,

{ Untitled, 1996, Jerry Uelsmann. }

Taylor photographed the landscapes of people's homes and yards, "suburban scenes with decrepit houses and fences and the weird yard art people would put out." Taylor's camera dwelled on the well worn and the thrown away, objects still redolent of their former uses, but separated from those who had used them. These photographs, while stylistically different from her current work, contain the germs of a lifelong project.

After graduating from Yale, Taylor moved around the East Coast between Boston and New York, and eventually followed a boyfriend to Palm Beach, Florida, where her parents had moved in 1980. For a while, she worked as a copyeditor at a newspaper, then as an administrative assistant at the Norton Gallery of Art. She kept photographing, using a darkroom her parents had let her set up in one of their bathrooms, and began applying to Master of Fine Arts programs.

Ultimately, Taylor chose the University of Florida, a haphazard choice, made more out of circumstance than because of any particular attraction to the program. Though she'd also been accepted at NYU, the University of Florida program in Gainesville offered her a job as a teaching assistant in art history. Culturally, it would take some getting used to. "I'd never been to this part of Florida at all. So I was a little upset when I saw the downtown. I thought, 'Oh my God, there are no tall buildings! Who would ever live here?'"

Gainesville is no Palm Beach: drive 15 minutes out of town in any direction and you're likely to hit a farm or a cattle ranch. But being out of the mainstream held certain advantages for the university's photography program, which had earned a reputation for unorthodoxy—due in large part to Jerry Uelsmann, a photography professor whose surreal black-and-white photographs melded images from several negatives onto one seamlessly constructed print. In the 1960s and '70s, Uelsmann's photomontages had generated excitement for a new photography that could be surrealist, metaphoric, and humorous all at once. He and other experimental photographers had spawned a new generation of artists who were playing with the medium in a more personal, unorthodox way. But none of that movement had reached Yale, and as far as Taylor's undergraduate program was concerned, the Florida program was off the radar. Still, the price was right.

Taylor's Yale mentors were dismayed that she'd chosen the University of Florida, even more so when she began to show them the work she'd begun to do there. Taylor had continued producing the urban landscapes she'd been interested in at Yale, but what brought her praise from the Florida faculty was a new series of still-life photographs, collections of family members and found objects she'd arrange in a tableau in a friend's backyard and photograph with a 4 X 5 camera in natural light. Taylor found new mentors in Gainesville, including Evon Streetman, a member of the University of Florida photography department who encouraged Taylor to work in color and to pay closer attention to details and lighting.

"People said 'This is good. You're branching out.' They liked the work because it seemed more personal and emotional. So I started taking the dolls and objects I'd collected at flea markets and photographing them. I could half-bury a doll, scatter letters around, make a little scene. My MFA show was just that: dolls, broken objects, old postcards, and my own drawings scattered around in the sunlight." The work was intimate, colorful, artificial—all of the qualities that had been discouraged at Yale. "I sent slides of this back to my Yale teachers and they wrote back and said things like 'It's interesting, and I can see that you're using your sense of humor, but it's not photography.'"

In many ways, this experimentation—and the rebuke that followed—were the genesis of the project that consumes Taylor today. Despite her formal photography training, Taylor has always balked at the limits of her craft. The Yale professors, says Taylor, "saw photography in a very narrow sense—that it was to show the real world. You know, with the slight shading and nuances of the photographer's eye, maybe, but the real world. And my work was not the real world. It was fabricated imagery. It was 'not photography.'" It was the same reaction she'd get years later, when she made the switch to digital art, but in both instances, Taylor was undeterred. (There's the *Moth dancer* again, hands on her hips.)

It wasn't just stubbornness: Taylor's new work was starting to be commercially successful. After a few shows at non-profit galleries around the country, dealers and commercial galleries were beginning to take note. The Houston Museum of Art and the Center for Creative Photography in Tucson bought prints. Since then, Taylor's photographs have been exhibited in more than 75 one-person exhibitions in the United States and Europe. Her work is in the collections at Princeton

University Art Museum; the Fogg Art Museum at Harvard University; Belgium's Musee de la Photographie; and the Museet for Fotokunst in Denmark, among many others.

Taylor was one of many photographers in the 1980s exploring the photographic potential of fabricated worlds. In Cindy Sherman's *Untitled Film Stills*, completed in the late '70s and early '80s, the photographer used herself as a model, impersonating various female movie archetypes. Like some of Taylor's own images, Sherman's film stills hinted at a larger, untold story, drawing on the viewer's own stereotypes and cultural references to complete the picture. Other photographers, many of them women, drew even more directly from the flotsam of mass media. Around the time Taylor started graduate school, Barbara Kruger was making photo-collages that reconfigured mass media advertising jargon into an anti-consumerist cultural critique. Meanwhile, Sherrie Levine challenged the ownership of images by "reappropriating" famous photographs in series like *After Walter Evans*.

Work like Sherman's and Kruger's forced art institutions to rethink the boundaries of traditional art genres—a curatorial challenge, but a conceptual one as well. Sherman's film stills were taken with a camera and printed in a darkroom, but the content of her photographs, with their narrative style and staginess, is painterly. The same description applied to Kruger's photography—a large print of which was displayed in the painting galleries at the Museum of Modern Art. (Likewise, the paintings of Gerhard Richter—and Andy Warhol's silkscreen prints before him—can seem more photographic than they do

{ Mood lifter, 2001. }

Often in Taylor's work, that thread tugs at childhood memories and impressions
the fear of the dark ; the sensation of being out of place;
deflated expectations; or sibling relationships.

painterly.) Just as the invention of photography had called into question its relation to other media, experimentation within photography was wearing at those boundaries even further.

It's easy to see how Taylor's work with Adobe Photoshop advances this march towards the collapsing of traditional artistic genres, though doing so is not her primary goal or interest. There's a strong element of photography in her work, both in her training and in her current technique. For example, the flatbed scanner that Taylor uses to capture various small objects and old prints functions much the same as a camera. She often uses a digital camera to photograph elements for her pieces (the headless torso in *Mood lifter* for instance, comes from a photograph Taylor took of herself). But the images that ultimately scroll from her printer are distinctly painterly, both in their lush, artificial colors and in the unreal scenarios they depict.

It was Uelsmann, whom Taylor married in 1989, who inadvertently initiated her into the world of digital photography. In 1995, a representative for Adobe approached Uelsmann to do a poster for the company using Photoshop. Adobe gave Uelsmann money to buy a state-of-the-art Macintosh computer and sent a Photoshop expert

named George Jardine to Gainesville, to teach Uelsmann how to use his new system.

With Jardine's and Taylor's help, the poster was produced, but that marked the end of Uelsmann's Photoshop foray. Taylor, on the other hand, was intrigued. "I thought I'd try to help Jerry," Taylor recalls, "so I sat down and read the entire manual." For two years she experimented with the software, creating images that she kept to herself. By 1998, she had nearly abandoned the camera, using a scanner instead, to "photograph" objects, letters, and old photographs and save them in her Macintosh, where she'd learned to combine and manipulate them in Photoshop. Uelsmann now had the darkroom to himself.

Working with Photoshop in this way can be as organizationally challenging as imposing the Dewey decimal system on a church basement book sale: it demands patience, perseverance, and a keen eye for distinctions. But computer work suits Taylor. "I've always liked desk jobs," she says. "I'm an excellent typist." There's a tidiness to Taylor, an efficiency, and love of details and organization. She relishes details and enjoys projects done right. One day I watched her tinker with a work-in-progress called *Girl with a bee dress*, which involved, at that point, a composite of six bees Taylor had found in her yard, each scanned in several different positions, then painstakingly tinted and shaded.

Perfectionism, persistence, and specificity go well beyond Taylor's computer work. Leland Shaw, a friend of Taylor and Uelsmann, touts her ability to cajole flight attendants into getting first class seats for her friends in coach. "You wouldn't call it obsessive," says Shaw, "you'd call it highly motivated. The rest of us walk around like, 'Whatever.' Maggie's always asking "What's better?" She simply excels at paying attention. Driving in Taylor's station wagon one day, the conversation turned to the relative merits of different cars' cup-holding devices. "There's a whole Web site devoted to car cup holders!" Taylor told me, with enthusiasm.

This is where Taylor resonates with the artist Joseph Cornell, whose box constructions showed a great appreciation for things that seem perfect and complete in their thing-ness, a near sanctification of seemingly quotidian objects. "I was into some things long after they were age-appropriate," she says. "I remember when I was 12; I got the Playskool airport because I thought the airplanes and the little helicopter were just so perfect. I loved these things, just as objects." Her studio today is filled with a spectacular collection of curios that line her shelves and drawers—a housecleaning nightmare. Among her collections are small die-cast chairs made by a defunct '30s company called Tootsie Toy, and what she describes as "very small people made for train sets; pigs that are small, and made of plastic, porcelain, metal; dolls that are very worn but have interesting bodies made of ceramic or composite material; wings from insects or birds; dead animals I find and put in our freezer." The objects are bought at flea markets and on eBay, and then considered and reconsidered, sometimes over a period of years as they "begin to develop a personality."

Objects like these appeal to her in the same way as the "decrepit houses and fences and the weird yard art"did when she was an undergraduate in New Haven. Taylor still avoids photographing people, but she has found a reliable cast of characters in the form of century-old tintypes and ambrotypes that she collects and scans into her computer. Like her well-worn toys and dolls, these long-dead faces are the detritus of human relationships, of childhoods grown out of, marriages celebrated and ambitions realized. They imply a history and a context, but they hold their secrets close.

In Taylor's hands these objects become protagonists of a new drama, one we only half understand. Describing her work, she has said: "I wish for the viewer to experience a convergence of factual memory and fictional daydream, similar to my own internal dialogue in creating the work." Exploring this internal dialogue and the process by which it is articulated is the project of this book. But the particular convergence Taylor describes—the story her subjects tell us—is the viewer's alone.

Not yet, 1998.

{ Maybe never, 1998. }

{ Small storm, 2002. }

{ Stray thoughts, 2003. }

{ Gorilla boy, 1999. }

Burn, 2000.

". . . I can't come to terms with what they're really about, but I can

find resonance in the way they make me feel. That feeling

is totally solitary and alone. Looking at art or reading a book is a totally

solitary experience. We do it alone, and the best response is sometimes that we

can't quite articulate how we feel."

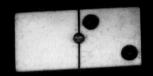

CHAPTER TWO

Eight Observations

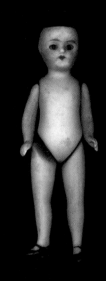

Paul Karabinis
The Stillness of Perfection

PAUL KARABINIS IS THE GALLERY DIRECTOR at the University of North Florida in Jacksonville. He's interviewed both Taylor and Jerry Uelsmann and has written extensively about Uelsmann's work.

Describing Taylor's pictures, he says, "Maggie's work is characterized by perfect stillness. I suspect this may have something to do with how she continually works over her images, making certain everything is exactly as she wants it to be. The gestures, poses, settings, and overall atmosphere in her work seem absolute, final, and perfectly preserved as if in an airless vacuum. I am not suggesting that her work relates in any way to the notion of the 'decisive moment' frequently associated with photography, but is rather a result of working with a picture-making process (the computer) that allows for a kind of execution or control that is just not possible in photography. Knowing Maggie as I do, the work also reflects her temperament with having everything as it should be. I think she is driven by a keen sense of order and perfection that manifests itself through a working and reworking of her images. This might be characterized as obsessive, but I see it as being driven by a desire to take full advantage of

{   A little careless, 1999.   }

the picture-making system she uses."

The chemical processes of darkroom work are often described as having an alchemic appeal, but to Karabinis, Taylor's computer work is just as ritualistic and mysterious.

"When I'm at Maggie and Jerry's, I'm working with Jerry, but Maggie's work is always around and available to look at. It is also very interesting to see her at the computer. Sometimes I look into her workroom and it's so dark I can't see anything but her silhouette illuminated by the glow of the monitor. It's a scene that is replete with symbolism that I should probably not venture into. I have also seen her work—finessing the keyboard and mouse with an effortlessness that suggests a connection with materials and process that all artists strive for. I do believe something does occur during that encounter she has with her computer and software that is as significant and revelatory as the experience we have always associated with the making of art."

Taylor can spend days adjusting the color levels on an image, moving in and out of grayscale to experiment with different hues. Sometimes a picture will remain in a state of incompletion for months because Taylor can't adjust the color to her liking. According to Karabinis, these colors are the lure.

"What initially draws me into Maggie's pictures is the lusciousness of their color. I am seduced by color, which is something that has always bothered me about color photography. With photographs, color seldom seems true or authentic. And it has frequently proved an obstacle to my enjoying a work. But I don't relate to Maggie's images as photographs. I see them as hybrid pictures hovering somewhere between painting and photography. As such, I suppose I don't hold them hostage to reality. I'm not sure how the color affects me, as once I begin moving through a picture, my attention shifts to the content and design. As indicated earlier, I am struck by how perfectly stilled her figures and objects appear, situated as they are within such lush and fantastic settings. It is difficult to say just what she's trying to do, but this is part of the charm of the work. I can't quite come to terms with any given piece. This sounds like a typical way of circumventing discussion about the work, but it's the way I generally respond to art. I'm attracted to works—books, movies, photographs, paintings—that I can't quite resolve or that simultaneously attract and confound me."

So what are we looking at when we look at Taylor's images? Whose story is this? Does the meaning of the image lie in Taylor's intent in making it, or in the interpretations we viewers bring to it? Those are questions we could ask of any piece of art. (And asking them, you could argue, is what it means to think about art.) Looking at Taylor's images, Karabinis sees both forces at work.

"I believe all pictures are self-images to some degree," he says. "But whatever meaning we find in an artist's work has to be personalized if it is to have any resonance with a viewer. Now, I'm not privy to Maggie's personal psychology, her needs or desires, but I have become aware of certain aspects of her personality that would be evident to anyone who gets to know her. There's an element of perfection and style and elegance in everything she does. And her works are characterized by these qualities as well. As I indicated earlier, her continual working and

reworking of these pictures is directed toward finding the exact arrangement, color, and nuance such that you get the feeling that what you're looking at could not have been visualized in any other way.

"Obviously there are elements in her work that have accrued meaning long before Maggie used them. Whether it's a nest or a bird or an egg or a boat, there is a symbolism that's probably understandable to all of us. For example, the egg is a Christian symbol of the resurrection. In secular terms it's a symbol of rebirth. And the boat is a symbol of passage or flight from one place or stage to another.

"But you've got to be careful applying such literal meanings to her work because where, then, do you go? If you start saying 'Well this picture with the boat is about transformation from one part of life to another,' or 'These eggs are about rebirth,' where does that really take you? Literal readings seldom lead us to any significant end. I'm less concerned in finding concrete meaning and more interested in where the process of engaging with the work can take me. Maggie's work frequently suggests something secret that can never be resolved. I know it has been said before, but a great part of the pleasure of engaging with an expressive work is that the experience is solitary and open-ended. The goal is less about finding answers than about achieving a condition that leads to more questions. I think you have to have a tolerance for ambiguity and a willingness to suspend yourself in that little world she has created in order to enjoy and appreciate these works. It's a secret world that has few guideposts but unlimited destinations—if we come to the work with a sense of wonder."

Alison Nordstrom
Actually Quite Dark

ALISON NORDSTROM IS CURATOR of Photographs at the George Eastman House in Rochester, New York. She spent 11 years in Florida as Senior Curator and Director of the Southeast Museum of Photography at Daytona Beach, where she met Uelsmann and Taylor.

"One thing I like about Maggie's work, obviously, is craft. We see a lot of bad Photoshop, and she is very good at it. But what I think is interesting about Maggie's images is that at first glance they are cartoon-like; they are funny, and I like that. There's not nearly enough funny going on in contemporary art. But once you get beyond the immediate surface of their sort of pop-like use of color and visual one-liners, there's something else going on that's actually quite dark. I think that's what I find most interesting about them: that although they appear to be very lighthearted, if you spend any time with them, you begin to see that there is a lot of other stuff going on.

"I wouldn't place her into a category of so-called 'Southern' photography, but it is interesting to think about the Florida landscape in relation to Maggie's work. Florida looks so sunny, but then it

{ Man pretending to be a rabbit, 2003. }

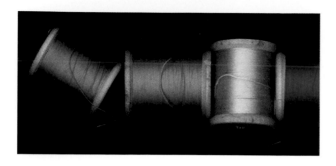

has this dark underbelly, and there's that element in her images. At first glance you think you're looking at something light and funny, but the deeper you look, the darker it gets. And you can't just take it and figure it out. It remains ambiguous, and that ambiguity is essential. In many cases I can almost imagine the novel that Maggie's images would be the color illustration for. I don't think they're one-liners. That's one of the reasons the work is strong—it is not code."

When Taylor first began sending her Photoshop work to galleries, she heard from many of them that the work wasn't photography and couldn't be shown and sold as such. That reaction is similar to the reaction Uelsmann's work provoked in the art world in the 1960s, when he began producing his multiple-negative images.

"Jerry's work is significant," Nordstrom says, "because he was making it at a time in photography when absolute high modernism was in charge. The basic belief was if you manipulated anything at all, you would die. If you cropped, you would go to hell. To be making the work he was making at that time, allied Jerry much more with the printmaking tradition than the photographic traditions of the '60s.

"Maggie is coming to us at a completely different time. And though I think she's in many ways as closely allied to the printmaking tradition as to the photographic tradition, there's always been a bridge area between the disciplines, and now disciplinary boundaries are blurred completely.

"There are people who are much more conservative within their own telling of photographic history, but we're losing them. And that's OK."

Nordstrom raises interesting questions: Should Taylor's images be classified as photography? Printmaking? Do we need a new genre? Does digital art signal the death of classical artistic taxonomy? Or are those questions not so compelling after all?

"The question of Photoshop is one that we have to address, but it matters less and less. We have to think about how we define photographs now that they're not about film anymore, but that's true of every photograph we deal with. And that's sort of a wonky, museum issue; it shouldn't matter to most people.

"People have been using whatever techniques were at hand to make photographs look different from how they would look if it was just a straight photographic process since the beginning of photography. Daguerreotypes were hand painted. Lots of people in the nineteenth century were printing multiple negatives to get a look, or smearing petroleum jelly on their negatives to get a look that they couldn't get any other way. So the issue is, 'Is it a photograph or not?' It's increasingly difficult to make that distinction, but I would argue that most people understand Maggie's work as a manipulated photograph."

Trudy Wilner Stack
A Romanticized Sense
of Past

TRUDY WILNER STACK IS AN INDEPENDENT
curator, editor, and writer. From 1992 to 2002,
she was curator at the University of Arizona's Center for Creative Photography where she was introduced to Maggie Taylor and her work. Wilner Stack
was born the same year as Taylor, 1961, and owns
an early picture taken by Taylor when she was still
working in traditional photography.

"I wrote in my notes for this interview: 'Man
Ray meets Joseph Cornell at the writing desk of a
Victorian woman.' Maggie embodies the spirits of
all three of these references and more.

"There is the private world of the journal
keeper and the collector. And then there is the
montagist, the surrealist player whose tools are
juxtaposition and dislocation. Then there's the
painterly quality; one of the things digital imaging
brought Maggie when she evolved from traditional
photography to Photoshop was the physical medium of pigment. Her prints became richly adhered
compositions of powdery pigment on paper and not
glassy emulsion-coated light-sensitive studies—and
that's very different."

Taylor may use contemporary tools, but Wilner

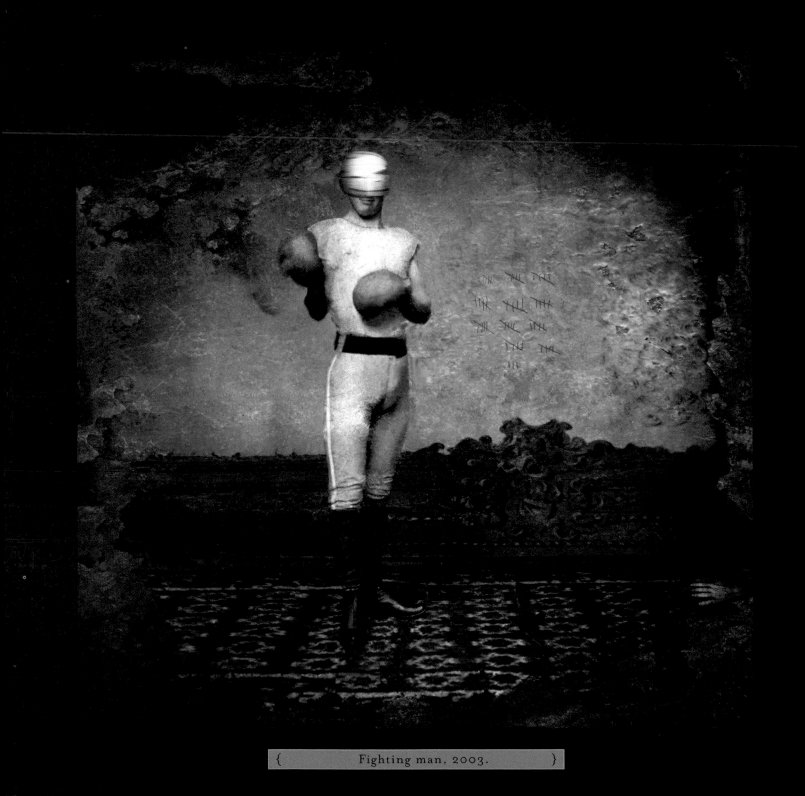

{ Fighting man, 2003. }

Stack sees in Taylor's work a sympathy with nineteenth century sensibilities, especially those of Victorian women who found artistic expression in the domestic arts, like album-making and sewing. Taylor will like this analogy. Among her collections are a handful of nineteenth century lithographs, hand painted, as Taylor points out, "by women working by the light of whale-oil lamps." From searching eBay for tintypes to hand-coloring her images in Photoshop, digital tools give Taylor access to both a vocabulary and an approach that are unique in nature.

"She is using a very sophisticated piece of technology that one can liken to photography in its most elemental form: the scanner. In principle, its direct reading of the object it records is a pure and literal rendering, as is the elemental photogram. The photogram, one of photography's earliest and most unmediated manifestations, is made by simply laying the subject on light-sensitive paper and exposing it to light to describe its exact outline and its contours if it has any transparency."

The photographer, painter, sculptor, and filmmaker Man Ray introduced photograms—or Rayographs as he called them—in the 1930s to Dadaists and Surrealists with his images of natural and electrical objects, many from a series commissioned by a French electricity company. But, as Wilner Stack points out, the fascination with photograms dates back much further, to photography's infancy.

"In the nineteenth century, photograms were very popular because they didn't require a camera or a lens. People used photograms to capture leaves, feathers, shells, and stones—the handy leavings of natural history. This recalls Maggie's practice to me. The scanner works similarly to a photogram if you think about it. You lay the actual objects down to make a direct imprint of them. There's no intermediary stage, no negative or transparency; it's a literal take. The chief distinction is that the photogram provides only the silhouette of an opaque object, and the scanner provides full detail and color. But the principle is connected and relevant.

"It gets back to those journaling women of the late nineteenth century. They pressed and sketched flowers to illustrate the walk in the woods they also described in words. They wrote vivid letters to summon the details of their experience in the world—the quality of pale color borne by a robin's egg or the enticing smells of a baking pie. These were not trivial observations of events and surroundings that had only private signification; these were careful and sincere elucidations of the quotidian, the everyday that defined these women—the everyday they creatively interpreted and preserved as precious.

"Maggie forsakes full narrative for a more cryptic, unmoored, and symbol-driven method of empowering her subjects with meaning. The complexity of twenty-first century life, including the barrage of images and ideas and consumer opportunities presented by popular culture, can overwhelm and ultimately add up to very little. It seems that Maggie is drawn back into a complexly romanticized vision of the past where a bit of cut hair or other keepsake could encompass a universe of emotion and meaning."

Joseph Cornell, the renowned filmmaker, collagist, and assemblage artist, who died in 1972

Fading away, 2004.

and is perhaps best known for his boxes in which he arranged photographs and bric-a-brac, had a similar love for and fascination with objects—many of which, on their own, would have looked quite ordinary to anyone else. Like Taylor, he had a great interest in Victoriana and in objects from the natural world: bird feathers, nests, and seashells. Also like Taylor, he maintained a vast library of objects and images in his home studio, and based his artwork on the ideas they inspired in him.

"The collecting impulse is an important piece for Maggie Taylor. Obsessive collectors risk the danger of being overrun by the objects they amass. What then? There are many examples of collectors whose extraordinary collections exceed their limits and are sold or donated to clear the way for new things. Taylor's art allows her to create something out of the impulse to collect; her collections feed her art and are transformed by her practice. They can never be static.

"Her various images add up to a much larger expression. They are seemingly alike and overlapping, as though a constantly evolving singular series. But series is an inadequate word; hers is a more literary project, epic in its proportions when taken together. While each image functions well in isolation, they are also scenes to successive chapters. When her images are too similar, they can undercut each other. These are essentially variants of the same idea and shouldn't necessarily be seen together. But with a strong edit they do different things and compound and strengthen Maggie's unique vision where her other world firmly takes shape."

That other world may contain historical objects but, says Wilner Stack, Taylor's images are ahistorical; her figures are characters in a drama that has no obvious place in time.

"I wouldn't say Maggie Taylor's work is any less contemporary; I'd say it is not contemporary in its content but in its intent. She doesn't tend to literally reference the now; rather, she subverts the past in order to redeem the present.

"Her early, pre-digital, photographs were constructed of what looked like photographed things, like an arrangement of things that had been photographed. With her digital technique, you can no longer unravel how the image was made. It simply exists. That mystery is key to the seductive power of her work.

"While her compositions are made up of familiar elements, familiar triggers, their whole is something completely new. You find yourself entering someone else's dreams—or other imaginings or summonings that are not your own. As with good fiction, you are transported to a place outside yourself, provocatively estranged from your own perceptions and fantasies. But once seen, Maggie's images can infiltrate and influence the dream state of your next sleep like the best of suggestions."

Jerry Uelsmann
Why Compromise?

J

JERRY UELSMANN TAUGHT PHOTOGRAPHY to a generation of artists at the University of Florida in Gainesville, among them Maggie Taylor. Uelsmann's photographs combine negatives into a dreamlike, some say surrealistic image, that is produced as a traditional silver gelatin print.

"Before Maggie came to Gainesville, she studied photography at Yale, which had a much more conservative, less experimental program," Uelsmann says. "Believe me, they never would have discussed my work at all there. She ended up coming here for grad school for practical reasons, since she was a state resident and it would have been much more expensive to go to a school in New York or elsewhere.

"When Maggie started her MFA at the University of Florida, her first images were unaltered, 'straight,' almost documentary. Our program was much more integrated with the larger art department. Students could work on projects in several areas at once: photography with painting or sculptural elements. As teachers, we were trying to get people to create imagery that related to their personal experiences. Maggie began exploring

{ Southern gothic, 2001. }

We threw our Brussels sprouts behind the radiator, 1986.

fabricated imagery using old family snapshots and cryptic objects. She photographed with a large-format camera and printed in color. The documentary work wasn't bad work, but I think she discovered she was more excited about inventing realities for herself.

"In some cases the photographs were playful and autobiographical. I remember a story about how her father hid Brussels sprouts behind the radiator because he didn't want to eat them. Stories would come back from childhood. They had a kind of personal, narrative quality. You could still respond to the images without knowing the specific narrative, but the images all had poetic, story-like implications. It wasn't just an arrangement of things that was addressed to the eye. There was this feeling that you wanted to think about these things."

Looking at Taylor's early, pre-Photoshop work, you can see how she strains against the limits of conventional photography, or the "photography gods," as Paul Karabinis once referred to them. Natural light is unreliable, and the laws of physics impose their own logic. Uelsmann recalls Taylor's frustration with her pre-digital methods: "When she was photographing her still-life fabrications with a view camera, making traditional four-inch by five-inch color transparencies, there was always an element of frustration with the technical aspects. She would expose multiple sheets of film for each set-up, moving an object or changing the angle of light just a little each time. It gets to be rather expensive to take all that film and get it processed. She'd get it all developed and then say 'Well, if that object were only over further to the left.' Then she'd set the scene up and start all over again on another day. So in a sense, it was that frustration of trying to strive for something that she had greater control over that led her to be interested in the computer. She saw the potential of being able to move things around and finesse them in ways she never could before."

Taylor's office is at the back of the house, near the patio that leads to Uelsmann's studio. If Uelsmann has his music up loud, Taylor heads over to complain. Over the course of the day, the two will drift in and out of each other's workspaces many times, casually surveying the other's progress. Often Uelsmann will make suggestions about the composition of one of Taylor's images; that a boa of seaweed, for instance, be draped around a woman's neck. But that sort of feedback doesn't work both ways.

"These days, when Maggie looks at my work she'll make little suggestions for changes or subtleties that would be impossible in the darkroom. I can't suddenly eliminate a tree that I don't like, and she *can* do that. If I'm honest, I am a little bit jealous of the complex things she can do with the computer.

"When people ask me to talk about working digitally, one of my standard replies is, 'Say something good about the computer: it gives you an immense number of visual options. Say something bad about the computer: it gives you an immense number of visual options.' The fact that I have more limited choices, in a sense, helps me. There's always a point at which you've got to make decisions in order to move forward creatively. With the multitude of digital techniques available, decisions are much more difficult.

"As humans we're conditioned to strive toward the best possible outcome. As artists, we want each image we make to be perfect. But practically speaking, there's a point at which you must try to resolve the concept and move forward. And whether it's invented or real there's a point at which you think, 'It's time to move on to the next project.' You cannot spend the rest of your life finessing just one image.

"On the other side of that argument, I do believe that one of the wonderful aspects of making art is that it cannot afford compromise. So many things in life require us to compromise; that's a reality. But if you're working by yourself and you've got a blank piece of paper and you're creating something, why would you compromise? You want to make it the best you possibly can."

I asked Uelsmann for his favorite Taylor image. "I've always been particularly fond of *Southern gothic*, with the woman tearing her head apart. It has so many interesting psychological layers. On the one hand, tearing a head apart has the potential of being fairly gory. But the way it is presented, it has a much more poetic, metaphorical implication. It's not scary or frightening in any way. There's a self-discovery thing happening there. And when you think of a person literally tearing her head apart—I think it's rather fascinating that that's not what the image communicates. Also I like the way in which the woman becomes part of the landscape, with her skirt melting into the ivy at the bottom.

"I have lived here in North Florida since 1960, and I have come to love this dense, humid landscape. There's a reality beneath the surface reality that is waiting to be discovered. Chance events in our daily lives often provide sources for visual exploration. An insect in the garden, a frog on the fence, a forgotten image from a trip decades ago—all have the potential to become a source of inspiration. I am not sure how this fits in, but Maggie is a passionate gardener and has spent many hours nurturing plants and reconfiguring our landscape (not to mention our house)."

Uelsmann and Taylor's images look quite different and are made by entirely different means. But both pose conundrums that they don't completely answer. Uelsmann says that the meaning of these images is partly in the eyes of the beholder.

"People can look at these images and come up with personal interpretations. Much of contemporary art—and this is certainly true of Maggie's work and of mine—is really directed toward the creative consciousness of the viewer. It's not just a matter of making out what's there. The viewer must, on personal terms, deal with the image. Almost all of Maggie's images suggest a narrative; I can't think of one that doesn't. It may be nebulous, but a narrative suggestion or thread exists throughout her work. And no matter how dreamlike it may be, you are drawn into a personal dialog with the image.

"I've always felt that the visual arts are in a weak position as communication. Seldom do two people come away from viewing a painting or a photograph with exactly the same emotional and intellectual impact. But images are very powerful in the sense that you can experience works of art for a brief amount of time and have them stay with you for the rest of your life. There are deep and mysterious ways in which certain images resonate with your persona."

One of the most important lessons of her MFA program, Talyor says, is that in order to be an artist, one must keep making art. Visiting her and Uelsmann's house, I'm struck by how hard they both work. Each morning, after a cup of coffee and half an hour with the newspaper, they're off to their respective studios, where they'll remain until evening. Art making is their job, and both Taylor and Uelsmann take the labor seriously.

"Many people have the impression that an artist has dramatic moments when lightning strikes and they are suddenly inspired. The truth, for us, is that working on a regular basis creates conditions that help foster the creative process. Maggie and I both devote many hours each week to pursuing our visual quest. She is at the computer or looking through collections, I am in the darkroom or perusing my contact sheets trying to find a point of departure. We often meet in the late afternoon to see what the other person is working on, and we become the first audience for each other's images and ideas as they appear in their embryonic stage.

"We are constantly collecting source material, and in recent years we have found that we can share the objects to be scanned or photographed. For example, recently we discovered a bird that had evidently hit one of our windows and met an untimely end. Within a few minutes, Maggie had scanned the bird, and I set up a camera and tripod to record it on film. These images may or may not be used, but they become a part of each of our visual libraries."

Julieanne Kost
Permission to Make Believe

J

JULIEANNE KOST'S OFFICIAL TITLE is Adobe Evangelist; it's her job to spread the digital art gospel through workshops, literature, and coaching. But she's also an artist and a longtime friend of Taylor's. I asked Kost to name her favorite Maggie Taylor image.

"*Poet's house*. It's a relatively simple piece, but that simplicity raises big questions for me. Is the poet prolific? Are these finished pieces that he or she is happy with, or are these unsuccessful attempts at work? Is it a continuous stream of consciousness or are they individual works? Are these fleeting ideas since forgotten that have now flown out the window?

"It's a perfect representation of what a child would picture if a grownup said, 'He writes so much, it's like poetry is flying out of the house.' There's an air of fantasy about it even though the papers themselves seem quite real. I love the fact that Maggie still gives herself permission to make believe.

"I also thoroughly enjoy her color palette. It's intimate and warm and draws you in to the piece. It defines an age to the contents and feels very organic in terms of medium. I think that's what is most interesting about her work—she's making very organic, natural, from-the-heart work through a digital medium. [The work] doesn't *feel* digital at all."

That an image feels too digital is a common criticism of Photoshop-generated images, particularly from those who focus on traditional photography. It's a peculiar kind of criticism, finding fault in an art work on the grounds that it too closely reveals its medium. (Imagine someone objecting to a painting that "feels too painterly" or a piece of pottery that "feels too clay-like.") But digital imaging is still finding its place in the broader landscape of contemporary art. I asked Kost which artistic tradition she sees Taylor's work fitting in to.

"It depends. I know I hate that answer when other people say it to me, but I think it's very true in this case. If the 'tradition' of photography consists of capturing light, then yes, it's traditional photography. However, the way she's going about this task strays considerably from that tradition, and I think that's what makes it so interesting. There is a very different feel to a scanned object than you would get from a photograph, and the rest of her workflow—compositing images, changing elements and colors, etc.—is a blend of traditional techniques and new ways of achieving a result. Her work has evolved while digital imaging has helped her hone that style and vision, not become a crutch or a distraction.

"This stigma [of digital artwork] has been around before in other forms. Painters looked at early photographers the same way. I think it's largely a generational issue. The advent of any kind of new technology has a certain threatening feel to it, especially for people who are accomplished in that particular field. But looked at from another angle, it encourages exploration in other areas.

Photography caused painters to turn away from realism into more abstract approaches that weren't possible with a camera. For photography, it is that the entire process has changed in about 15 years. The capturing of images, the manipulation or adjustment of images, and the ways in which it is delivered has completely changed, and I think that is the primary issue people have with it. If we were simply to create a high-tech dodge tool for a dark room, there wouldn't be as much change to contend with.

Ultimately, I think work should be judged on the content in it, not the tools used in its construction. Maggie's work began long before she ever laid hands on a computer, so I think she's being true to what she wants to express and not relying on a computer to get her there."

It's often said that the problem with making art in Photoshop or other digital imaging software is that is too easy, that the abundance of effects and the ease of making major changes in color or composition take the challenge and thus, the logic goes, the authenticity or value out of an artwork. Taylor and Kost disagree: Photoshop demands great skill and craft, and anyway, why should the value of a piece of art depend on how it's made? Still, Kost agrees that the graphic possibilities of digital software can be distracting to a digital artist.

"The biggest challenge is knowing when you're done. With so many options, so much flexibility, and with exploration being so quick, it's tough to stop running through ideas and step back to ask

{ Poet's house, 1999. }

yourself, 'Have I said what I set out to say?' Maggie has been incredibly flexible and has always been willing to try something new. Technology is changing so quickly these days that it can be frustrating, but the key here is to get in as soon as you can and learn what you can. It's moving forward with or without you.

"When I look at Maggie's images, I see beautiful work. The individual techniques blend together into something much bigger. She has a firm technical grasp on Photoshop so there isn't a spot where I say, 'Ah! She didn't feather that selection quite enough!' She's mastered the techniques she needs,

allowing her to focus on communicating."

Finally, I asked Kost what kind of example Taylor's work sets for both the aspiring and the accomplished digital artists. "She brings her traditional training and expertise into a cutting-edge workflow. I think there's a tendency to leave tradition behind in favor of MTV-style imagery. So, for aspiring artists, I think it's important to see what's possible in a digital medium, but learn the rules before you break them. For accomplished digital artists, don't forget to get out the finger paints now and again and get your fingers dirty. Above all, play, play, play!"

Peter Bunnell
Floating Strawberries

PETER BUNNELL IS A PROFESSOR EMERITUS at Princeton University and a former curator of photography for the Museum of Modern Art. His writing includes books and essays on the work of John Pfahl, Edward Weston, and Jerry Uelsmann.

"Taylor's images are essentially non-reality based, which is, I think, both an imaginative and a positive use of the computer technology," Bunnell says. "There is no ambiguity as to whether or not these people, things, or creatures exist in this combination. In this sense, it is almost the direct opposite of her husband Jerry's work, where you have a tension, or a question, as to whether or not the pictured image could really exist whole. This is because his images rely so strongly on reality photographs—image fragments taken in context, in the world, with a camera and lens. Taylor has moved to a different place."

Bunnell sees in Taylor's work autobiography as well as a sense of her own wit and whimsy, and clearly an element of feminist or women's perspective. For starters, I see this in the abundance of women as subject matter. Also, the episodic quality to the pictures in which these women find

{ Woman with swan, 2002. }

themselves in terms of a kind of implied narrative, would seem to be one about themselves, and by extension, about Maggie. So it seems to me that they come very much from a woman's perspective.

"The Princeton Art Museum has three of Maggie's images from about ten years ago, when she was already using found artifacts or appropriated objects, which she assembled into still-lives and then photographed in the outdoors." (The seagull skull that appears in several pieces was a gift from Bunnell.) Those early still-lives very often had qualities that you more or less associate with a female perspective, in the sense of the mystery, the diaristic, and even the delicacy of them.

"In the nineteenth century, women frequently made albums of photographs, cut photographs, and pieces of cloth, with watercolor borders and that kind of thing; this was a preoccupation of upper middle class Victorian women. It is also interesting what the albums reflect of the status of women. The makers of the albums are usually anonymous. Sometimes we can make out the identity of the maker by virtue of the identity of the men in the album, but the women are generally unknown."

Bunnell is one of the few critics I spoke with who downplays the influence of Surrealism on Taylor's work. "It's not to say that there isn't an aspect of surreality in her pictures, but the tension that you recognized back in the high days of Surrealism—if you think of a cross between Man Ray and Salvador Dali—you can see that in each case, the images hovered between being hyper-real and surreal. I do not think that happens in Taylor's case. It's pretty much on one side, the unreal. Also, much

surrealist theory was erotic and anti-feminist, so it makes sense that she's not playing into that whole thing, though she's certainly aware of it."

Bunnell is a self-described luddite whose studies are rooted firmly in the realm of traditional photography—an ideal critic for Taylor's work, which he admires despite the high-tech medium she works in.

"There aren't very many people who are working as successfully in making images that are beyond mere bizarre juxtaposing with electronic digital imaging, what my students call 'floating strawberries.' They are not even surreal because they seem to lack any kind mystery or any kind of intelligent, psychoanalytic base. They are just weird."

"It is almost like a bunch of teenagers forming a rock band, but they don't have any ideas about musical content, just noise and instruments. The technology is too facile. It is predicated on making things that otherwise couldn't be made, so right away you start with a sense of the artificial, before you even turn the computer on. That's the difference between old photography and new photography. In old photography, you had to engage the world; if the subject didn't exist, and you didn't discover it and have a reaction to it, it wouldn't find a place in the photograph. With Photoshop, everything is up for grabs.

"Maggie's pictures do not look like other pictures—even those made in a similar fashion. It's not just that she has this bird skull and does this or that thing with it; there is a definite identity to what she does with it. It separates her from the pack through the force of her personal vision."

Mark Sloan
Out of Bounds From Language and Logic

Mark Sloan is the Director and Senior Curator for the Institute of Contemporary Art at the College of Charleston in South Carolina. He's also the author of several books, including his latest, *Hoaxes, Humbugs and Spectacles.*

"My wife and I own *Philosopher's daughter,*" Sloan says. "I have spent many pleasurable hours staring at that image. What I like is that its meaning continues to slip away just as I might feel I'm coming to some logical resolution. I like this slippery effect. I cannot explain what the image is in words. If I could, I would probably lose interest in it as an image. The image reaches part of my humanity that is out of bounds from language and logic. I think this is the terrain in which Maggie Taylor's work exists—the realm of the purely imaginary.

"Because I know Maggie, and I've heard her lecture about her work, I'm aware that certain elements of these images are deeply personal and autobiographical. Yet that does not matter to me. I see her work existing in the vapor of disembodied ideas. Maggie Taylor's imagery recalls for me the writings of Jorge Luis Borges, Fernando Pessoa, and Italo Calvino. She is creating ciphers that elide

{ Philosopher's daughter, 1999. }

(MAN IN HIS OWN WORLD, DETAIL)

specific meanings yet pertain to all of us in some way. There is a familiar and approachable aspect to the specific elements within a given image, yet her combinations create an uneasy tension, inviting the viewer to untangle the web of associations. The resulting untanglings will be different for each viewer. So, as with all the other great works of art, her works resist specific interpretation.

"This realm she has created (which is quite a feat!) has its own internal logic that is another of the appealing things about her work. It is as if each image one sees in her oeuvre informs our response to all that come after it. There is a certain self-referential quality that pervades the series of images. In seeing a grouping, one looks for clues and repetitions of elements or motifs."

I asked Sloan if there were other artists he's reminded of when he looks at Taylor's work. "Well, Magritte springs to mind—and the Surrealists. I suppose this link is unavoidable in the mode of work Maggie has chosen to pursue. I also see the link with Jerry Uelsmann's work, which I see in the choice of individual symbolic elements and in the preference for center-loaded compositions. I do not think any of these influences are over-powering or direct, however. Again, I think the work Maggie produces springs from a well of associational possibilities she has been collecting all her life. Good artists borrow; great artists steal—to steal a quote attributed to Picasso (though he probably stole it himself)."

Amy Kiser
A Spider's Victim Wrapped Tight

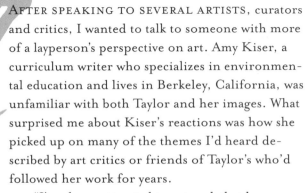

AFTER SPEAKING TO SEVERAL ARTISTS, curators and critics, I wanted to talk to someone with more of a layperson's perspective on art. Amy Kiser, a curriculum writer who specializes in environmental education and lives in Berkeley, California, was unfamiliar with both Taylor and her images. What surprised me about Kiser's reactions was how she picked up on many of the themes I'd heard described by art critics or friends of Taylor's who'd followed her work for years.

"I'm always attracted to artwork that has a narrative, that looks like it contains the whole of a story in it. That's why I'm not big on abstract art. These images look like they contain an entire story in them. They remind me of folktales or *Through the Looking Glass* kinds of things. I also like animal-people. There's something ancient or dreamlike about them—maybe that's because I see animals as people anyway—so whenever that idea is pushed, I like it.

"Some of these images also remind me of the narrative of a creepy dream, which is part of what I get from old photographs, like daguerreotypes. It wasn't typical for people to smile in old photographs;

Just looking, 1999.

everyone had a poker face. And that made everyone look like they were tragic somehow.

"It's interesting that this work is so rooted in computers—both in the way she gets the objects off eBay and how she makes the images in Photoshop. That's strange, because the objects she's working with seem like such textured, tactile things to me. They would have smell; old photographs smell, dust, the smell of old dolls, the smell of dead birds and skulls and feathers. Her stuff is everything I associate with a really olfactory or very sensory experience."

In talking with Kiser, I became curious about the image of Maggie Taylor that one might construct based on looking at her images. Taylor has many images of children, several of them, like *Strange beast* and *In a quiet room*, feature headless children, alone in environments that look empty but suggest some greater looming menace. Kiser was struck by this

apparent interest in the darker or more mystical aspects of childhood, and in what she called a "fragile, dreamy, gothic sensibility."

"It seems that she plays a lot with a theme of innocence, both in terms of how she uses animals, and the photographs of children. It's as if she's looking at childhood and what she sees is kind of sad or dangerous somehow. There's a sense of dreams and memories and hauntings that are in fiction or folktales or in the incredible, like circus sideshows.

"Take *Fragile*. It's a child, and what's coming out of her mind is… she doesn't look happy about it. It's as if she unburdening something loaded or heavy. It's like what the air feels like before a storm: high barometric pressure.

"A few of these images have overtones of sexuality. *Just looking*, for instance. It looks like a big, scary, sharp, dangerous schoolmarm examining a naked lady, as if she cold peck that naked lady with her big sharp beak and just eviscerate her. And the little woman has a ladder that could be her escape, but it doesn't go anywhere.

"The gothic or Victorian sensibility of these is about a fragility that's about to burst over. Barely contained. Like a spider having wrapped up its victim really tight."

{ Strange beast, 2003. }

{ Dreamer, 2003. }

{ The reader, 2002. }

{ Life goes on, 2002. }

{ Birthday boy, 2003. }

{ Rabbits with scissors, 2003. }

{ The butterfly hunter, 1998. }

"*The egg, that perennial symbol of maternal and artistic creativity,*

has a hold on Taylor, as it did on Joseph Cornell 50 years ago.

Masks, blindfolds, clouds, and faces blurred

out of recognition may be references to a sensation of alienation

or a desire to be invisible."

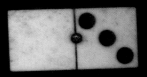

CHAPTER THREE

From Inspiration to Image

Inspiration Past and Present:
Heading Towards Image

WHEN IT IS TIME TO WORK, Taylor walks into her office, a small carpeted room facing the back of the house, and closes the blinds. The office, which doubles as a guest room, looks like the office of any work-at-home person, except for the large Epson flatbed scanner near the desk and the mishmash of seemingly unrelated knickknacks—military medals and tintype photographs, feathers and antique lithographs—clustered around the keyboard. Taylor turns on her desk lamp, sits down in her Aeron chair, and puts her hand on the rollerball mouse. The only sound in the room is the hum of her Macintosh G5 tower.

Taylor's computer is the primary instrument of her craft, and she regards it with the same affection and seriousness with which a painter might consider her easel or a ceramist his kiln. At the same time, Taylor knows that her chosen machine—unlike the kiln or the easel—has sometimes brought a stigma to her work and that of other digital artists. "Most people relate to the computer in their everyday life as a desk tool," Taylor says. "You're in college writing papers, or you're at home paying bills using the computer, or doing email on the computer. I think

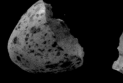

{ Adrift, 2005. }

people have trouble seeing how you could sit at it and use it in a totally creative way. It just so happens that I love sitting at a desk. It doesn't bother me that I might switch from typing a letter to someone to working on an image." Taylor uses her computer to shop for old photographs on eBay, to communicate with other artists and with her galleries, and finally, to make her images. "I love that all my work happens in one place."

Those who know Taylor are apt to point out that the way she works is a perfect fit for someone of her sensibilities. The work is sedentary, first of all, but it's also highly methodical, organized, and detail oriented. Sitting in front of her computer, Taylor is absorbed in the glow of its display, much as she was by her childhood television set. The scale of this work suits her, too. As a collector, Taylor is drawn to small things—dollhouse furniture, feathers, animal bones, old photographs—all of which fit neatly on a scanner. In Taylor's hands, even the limitations of Photoshop serve her purpose: the point at which a Photoshop-generated image looks too contrived or artificial, for instance, is the point at which Taylor may decide to make her own drawing. It's that resulting combination of the digitally constructed and the hand-hewn that gives her work its particular warmth and intimacy.

One work habit Taylor and her husband, Jerry Uelsmann, share is the need for solitude and, more importantly, *time* for an image to take shape. Traditionally, the creative moment in photography is the click of the shutter, the precise moment the photographer chooses to capture. In Uelsmann's work, that moment is postponed and prolonged, in the day-long darkroom process of combining and printing negatives. Similarly, Taylor often starts with a photograph or an image caught by a sweep of a flatbed scanner, but her craft is at the computer, frequently stretched over a period of months.

As a result, Taylor's creative process often looks like an endless series of mental switchbacks. "I think I like it better with just that one shark fin," she muses, her head cocked to the side, "but maybe there need to be three."

"You should call this book *Indecision!*" jokes Uelsmann, watching over Taylor's shoulder as she adds and then removes, and then adds and then removes, the element from her image.

What allows Taylor to suspend this period of creative indecision is a Photoshop technique known as "layering." Each element and effect Taylor adds to her image is saved as a separate layer, which lets her isolate that aspect and turn it on or off, experimentally. While Uelsmann's darkroom decisions are irreversible, Taylor's digital alchemy allows her to postpone decision making indefinitely. Until Taylor "collapses" her layers—a step that is ultimately necessary to shrink the file to a manageable size—every decision is elastic. The only point of no return for Taylor is when a print has been sent off to a gallery.

Some of Taylor's images take just a few days to complete; others span months. Occasionally, an image will reach a certain point and then stay there, suspended by Taylor's indecision or dissatisfaction with it. One image, tentatively titled *Girl with a bee dress*, sat in the folder for six months. "There was something I just didn't like about it," says Taylor. "I don't know, it was too pink. I loved the idea of

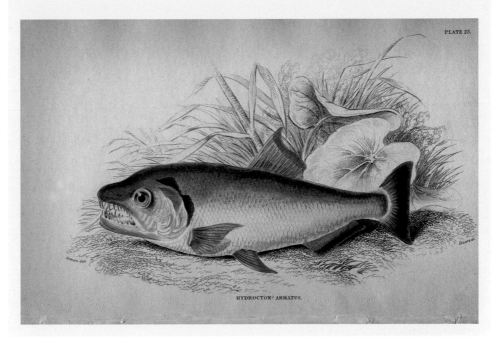

PLATE 25.

HYDROCYON? ARMATUS.

Taylor knows that her chosen machine—unlike the kiln or the easel—has sometimes brought a stigma to her work and that of other digital artists.

it, but it just wasn't working. So I set it aside." At the end of each year, Taylor revisits the folder to see which images she might see in a new light and complete, lest she begin the new year with last year's unfinished work.

Taylor produces about 12 to 16 finished images a year, in three sizes—8-inch, 15-inch, and 22-inch square. (The largest size, Taylor explains, is both the most difficult to print and the least popular with buyers. As a result, she's considering phasing it out of production.) In her first few years of working in Photoshop, Taylor sent her images to IRIS printers in Santa Fe and Clearwater, Florida. IRIS machines spray ink from tiny inkjet hoses onto paper wrapped around a 48-inch drum. It was the

industry standard at the time, but achieving the precise colors Taylor wanted was laborious; images would often have to be sent back and forth between Taylor and the IRIS technicians three or four times before the colors met her expectations. Then she worked for several years very happily with an IRIS printer in Rochester, New York.

Nowadays, Taylor prints at home on her Epson 9600, a table-sized inkjet (or "Giclee" as the galleries call it) printer that can produce images up to 44 inches wide. Looking at an inkjet print, Taylor is attuned to color saturation and black density, and to whether or not the ink will cling to the paper without flaking off and leaving tiny white specks across an image—a problem that has forced her to

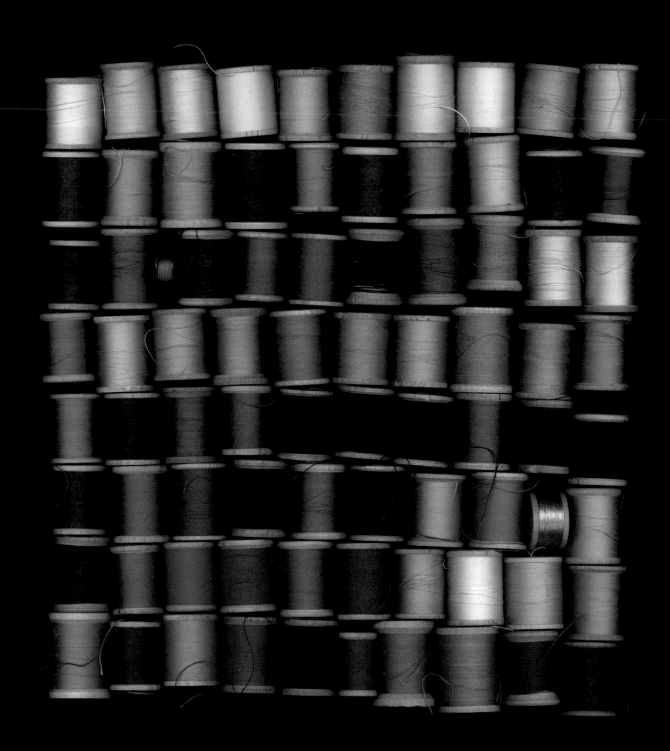

Sitting in front of her computer, *Taylor* is absorbed in the glow of its display,

much as she was by her childhood television set.

The scale of this work suits her, too. As a collector, *Taylor* is drawn to small things—

dollhouse furniture, feathers, animal bones, old photographs—all of which fit neatly

on a scanner.

recall prints from galleries in the past. These days, after experimenting with many brands of ink and paper, Taylor has found a combination of Epson inks and coated papers that gives her such reliable and color-saturated prints that—for the present—she no longer seeks improvements.

Longevity is another issue, and one that has nagged digital artists and color photographers since the beginning. Black-and-white gelatin silver prints (the standard among artists like Walker Evans and Ansel Adams) are permanent, unlike color photographs, which—depending on the materials used—can fade and color-shift, as most 70's family snapshots will attest. Inkjet prints are a recent enough technology that no one really knows how long they will last, though some inks have already proved to be short-lived. One batch of Taylor's images, printed on an IRIS machine in San Francisco, began to fade after only a few years. "I didn't sell any of those, thank goodness," says Taylor. In the mid-90's, Henry Wilhelm, adviser to the Museum of Modern Art, took Kodak and Epson to task for misrepresenting the longevity of their inks, launching—with the help of a Guggenheim grant—a new field of research into image preservation. (Wilhem also convinced Corbis, owner of the vast Bettman photo archive, to build a sub-zero, underground film-preservation laboratory in western Pennsylvania.) Since then, life expectancy of printer inks has improved dramatically.

Still, Taylor and other digital artists have questioned whether all the talk about the longevity of digital prints amounts to much more than a red herring. "If you look back at people who have been selling watercolors for several hundred years," says Taylor, "no one says anything about the fact that they aren't archival. I find it annoying that people only brought up these longevity issues with regard to color photography in the 70's and 80's." In a 1998 interview, Therese Mulligan, then the director of the George Eastman House, voiced a similar frustration. Asked whether the longevity of digital prints might limit their value on the art market, Mulligan replied that the question seemed to her, "to obscure, in part, the real discussion that needs to take place in regard to the digital medium... For me, digital technologies are like any other medium in the hands of an artist. They are another way to get at a picture. And it is the picture that should be utmost in our minds."

Taylor puts effort into researching papers and inks and uses the best archival papers she can find. But still, she says, it's the now of the image that matters most. "I'd rather have it look fabulous for whatever time it can—20 years or whatever—than have it last 100 years and be a muted version of what I hoped to achieve, with no blacks and no saturation in the colors."

If any of Taylor's images can be traced back to a single inspiration, often that source is something pulled from Taylor's and Uelsmann's collections. Along with the thousands of curios lining Taylor's studio drawers and Uelsmann's office shelves, the two keep a collection of outsider art by artists like Jesse Aaron, a self-taught Gainesville sculptor whose wooden animal totems were inspired, according to Aaron, by a directive from God, and Earl Cunningham, a self-taught painter from Florida whom Uelsmann sought out and photographed in the 1970s. A bookshelf near their front door is filled with a collection of small metal and wooden sculptures representing Exu, the god who, according to the Afro-Brazilian Candomble religion, opens pathways and delivers messages. "Our friend Mario Cravo Neto told us Exu would chase away evil spirits if placed behind the front door," Taylor says.

What objects Taylor and Uelsmann don't actually collect, they're likely to collect books about. Flipping through a volume of *milagre ex votos*—small wooden dolls used in Brazil as prayers for healing various ailments—one day, Taylor was captivated by the carving of a scar line across the belly of one of the crude, but oddly expressive, wooden figures. "I need to remember that," she said. "I definitely want to use some kind of scar in one of my images." Taylor's work is full of this kind of recycling. Those die-cast blue Tootsie Toy chairs, for instance—one of Taylor's favorite collections—appear in *The blue train*, which was commissioned by New York City's Metropolitan Transportation Authority (and in one of Uelsmann's images, as well).

Many of the objects come from Taylor's own family, including a trove of memorabilia Taylor inherited after her grandmother died, like the thread collection Taylor uses as a color palette, a collection of perfectly preserved 1950s hats, and a childhood schoolbook illustrated with her grandmother's enigmatic World War I-inspired doodles, one of which appears in *Butterfly hunter*.

Taylor and Uelsmann both travel with cameras, which they use to take photographs that might be useful in future work. "Jerry is my role model for this," says Taylor. "When he's out traveling, he's collecting images for his visual library. Some of the things I know I can definitely use are water and cloud images. Textures too. Grass. Sometimes if there's an interesting wall with a nice texture on it. Those are all things I can use." Uelsmann also learned from a role model: Minor White, the Zen-inspired photographer of the natural world, who taught Uelsmann that, "One should photograph things not only for what they are, but for what *else* they are." That eye for the metaphorical resonance of an image or object is perhaps the strongest bond between Taylor's and Uelsmann's work.

That eye is what brings Taylor back time and time again to objects so rich in metaphor that her use of them often has more to do with instinct than with specific narrative purpose. The egg, a perennial symbol of both maternal and artistic creativity, has a hold on Taylor, as it did on Joseph Cornell 50 years ago. Nests and other remnants of avian life also appear frequently, as do other animal parts, often as appendages to human ones. Masks, blindfolds, clouds, and faces blurred out of recognition or simply removed from their bodies—all are recurring themes in Taylor's work as well, references, perhaps, to a sense of alienation or a wish to be invisible. Taylor suggests what she's after in these images, but she never makes it explicit. Her work, full of happy accidents and second guessing, makes room for her subconscious to assert itself, as a close examination of Taylor's process reveals.

Building a picture: *Twilight swim*

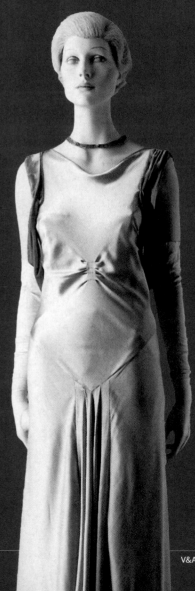

THE IDEA FOR TWILIGHT SWIM begins with a postcard from the Victoria and Albert Museum in London. The card depicts a simple mannequin modeling a silk dress and long gloves from the museum's collection. "It is a very simple gown that was like a blank canvas," says Taylor, recalling what drew her to this particular costume. "And it's also light, which is kind of unusual, because in the old tintype photos I have, everything is dark, black, or formal looking."

Taylor knows she wants to make an image of a woman standing in water, a concept she's worked with often in the past. "I like the idea of people dealing with their environment in a strange way," she says. "There's no one single meaning behind it. It could be with the sense of being a fish out of water, or that you're in an unfamiliar environment. It puts a different psychological spin on the image of the person, I guess. And in this case I want to revisit that idea."

Taylor scans the postcard into her computer and begins trimming the image of the dress from its background. Easy enough to do, given the simplicity of the picture. Next, she uses Photoshop's eraser tool to remove the woman's head from the figure.

With a rudimentary protagonist in place, it's time to begin building the background of the image. Like most of Taylor's backgrounds, creating this one will be a complex process ultimately involving a composite of seven layered images of water

FIGURE 3.5

FIGURE 3.6

photographs and several images of clouds and sky.

"I took one of these images of clouds with my digital camera at the beach. [In Photoshop] I put a hue and saturation adjustment layer over the photograph that affects it, but not permanently, so I can go back and change it if I want." Another overlay of clouds from a second photograph adds another color to the sky, and a warmer tone near the horizon.

The lower half of the image is composed of several photographs of water, taken with Taylor's four-megapixel Canon Elph at California's Mono Lake and Yosemite National Park. "There's a snapshot of the shore of a lake, that's why you're looking down at some rocks. I've made that layer partly transparent, so that you can see through to a different lake, because I thought by layering two snapshots of the lakeshore together, one being partly transparent on top of the other one, it kind of gives it a dreamlike effect that you're looking through somewhat murky water."

Taylor now adds a layer mask to the skirt of her figure, giving it a watery transparency, or as she describes it, "a little more visual confusion." She also makes some color adjustments with yet more layers.

At this point, Taylor has essentially completed the basic background of her image, a total of 11 layers, some of which contain actual pixel information, while others are only used for adjusting the color or opacity of images already in place. It's taken nearly

FIGURE 3.9

FIGURE 3.10

two full days of work. Other artists might now collapse the layers to make the file less cumbersome, but Taylor keeps her options open.

"I have a hard time making decisions, and I want to have the option to be able to go back still and tweak the color and change it. So I don't want to merge together all that background in the image at this point because I may go back and raise or lower the horizon line, for example, change the composition. As long as I have enough memory that I can deal with it in the computer—and I'm sometimes pushing the boundaries of that—I try to keep all the layers separate, to have the freedom to move them around. Because invariably, I come back after making a proof print and want to change it around again."

Next, Taylor paints in a thin white line at the point where the woman's body meets the water and begins to prepare another water layer to place on top of the woman's lower half. This time it's a photograph of a ripple in a Yosemite lake.

Taylor also fills out the woman's skirt by making a copy of it and stretching it out to the sides, as if the fabric has been caught and unfurled by a current. "In Photoshop you can change the dimension of something," explains Taylor, "and the stretched skirt is partly transparent—it's only 80 percent—so the effect is not too overwhelming." She also adds a darker layer around the woman's waist, like a watermark, where her dress has absorbed moisture.

Next Taylor paints in a moon and stars, and

FIGURE 3.11

pastes in a fish swimming to the woman's left. In the past she has scanned actual dead fish from Petsmart, but in this case the fish comes from an 19th century hand-colored etching that she scans and retouches. The final fish is a composite of several layers—some sharp, others blurry—to give it the appearance of watery motion. Still, it's not quite working. "I was concerned that the woman was maybe a little too off to the right and the fish was a little too big, and I just wasn't sure how they were working together. Also at this point I needed a head for her."

A good head is hard to find. Taylor looks for faces that are clear and easy to read. Often, if a face in an old photograph is too blurry or damaged, she'll blur it further, both as a time-saving Photoshop measure and as a depiction of self negation or confused identity. For *Twilight swim*, Taylor wants to use a woman's head with an expression ambiguous enough to adapt to her setting, which, like many Taylor settings, will come to include an element of lurking danger. Luckily, these poker-faced figures are common to 19th century photography, a consequence of primitive photographic technology, which required subjects had to sit frozen in place for a period of time.

After experimenting with several faces she

FIGURE 3.12

Taylor's digital alchemy allows her to postpone decision making indefinitely.

Until Taylor "collapses" her layers—a step which is ultimately necessary to shrink the file to a manageable size—every decision is elastic. The only point of no return for Taylor is when a print has been sent off to a gallery.

scanned in and extracted from old photographs, Taylor settles on that of a young girl from a 19th century tintype she bought on eBay. "I ended up liking this moony round quality of this face, but she didn't have good hair so I knew I'd have to add hair or add something else."

That problem spawns another day of work as Taylor labors to create a bathing cap that matches her memories of the 1960s rubber swim caps she saw (and used) in her youth. Taylor's first step is to draw the outline of the cap and then use a combination of Photoshop's pattern tool and distorting filters to create a wavy swim-cap pattern. But the result is too precise, too perfect. "I became kind of obsessed with it," she tells me later. "In the end, I hand-drew it, then used the Liquify tool to go in and work the individual lines a bit so that it's not perfect."

Also missing, by Taylor's estimation, is an element of uncertainty that will elevate this image from simple illustration to narrative. "I really need something in the distance, something to imply a certain danger, or something going on in the

distance that you aren't quite sure about."

This is the risky juncture, says Taylor, where Photoshop's freedoms can start to overwhelm and an image gets "too junked up." She adds several jumping fish to the background, along with two fish hanging like epaulets from the woman's shoulders. Using a new adjustment layer, Taylor then adds shading and color to her face, and some darkening around the picture's edge to give the image a more nocturnal feel. Next, she adds a seaweed necklace for the woman and gives the fish a pearl necklace.

"I feel like there needs to be some sort of dynamic relationship between the woman and the fish. I'm trying to understand her relationship to the water. I think maybe she needs a seaweed necklace, something as if she's just come out of the water, like she belongs in the water. Not quite a mermaid, but kind of like the idea of the mermaid."

"It just makes sense that if she's got some water elements, then the fish should have some dressy human elements, but I don't want to put a human face on the fish. I tried the necklace, but at that point I realized it was just too busy, too much going on and

FIGURE 3.13

FIGURE 3.14

I needed to simplify. These stages are a struggle, but they have to happen."

In an effort to simplify, Taylor shrinks the fish, turns off the layer of its pearl necklace, and eliminates the jumping fish in the background. She evens the color on the woman's face to give her a moonlit look, and begins to re-think the image. To her mind, it's still missing that critical element of drama. The challenge is to add narrative without adding obviousness or cliché.

One solution that comes to mind is replacing the jumping fish with shark fins. To that end, Taylor uses Photoshop's drawing tools to draft a master shark fin and then three slightly different iterations of it, flipped to appear as if circling the woman. The shark fins, each with its own drawn shadow and a "little white ripple where it hits the water" take up another 18 layers on the image. With this much laboring, she finds herself growing attached to the fins, despite some ambivalence over the direction the image is taking. "It's scary, because you don't want to make things that are too cliché or too corny or too much like an illustration. So in a way I like the version of this image without the shark fin. But in the end I have to decide which one I want to make a finished print of." Later she says, "I ended

up liking the one with the shark fin. Still, it's a very hard decision to make."

Next, she adds another necklace of seaweed, built from the scans of real seaweed that Taylor has brought home in a cooler from Longboat Key.

But there remains one unresolved problem with the image: "If the shark is that big, shouldn't you see a shadow or part of the body of the shark?" Well, maybe, or maybe not. But the idea is worth exploring, which Taylor does, then comes to a decision: "I won't show the bodies of the sharks, instead, I'll add a fin to the underwater fish. That will put a new spin on it."

With that one small adjustment *Twilight swim* is complete. Taylor prints it and sends it with a batch of images for a show in Houston. Looking at the piece a month later, she's pleased at how that final, small adjustment both completed and changed the image. "Putting the fin on the fish makes it less menacing, maybe. But you still don't know. You don't know if these are real sharks and this fish is just protecting himself, and therefore, if she is still in danger. Or, if all the sharks are not so bad and that's why she's so nonchalant; they're all just fish with fake shark fins." It's just the kind of ambiguity Taylor was after all along.

{ Twilight swim, 2004. }

Work in Progress

> *Moth dancer*

> *Man with too much time*

> *Surrounded*

> *Girl with a bee dress*

Moth dancer

MOTH DANCER BEGINS with a tintype Taylor bought on eBay. First, she removes dust spots and irregularities from the image and changes to a square format. Next, a makeover: the child gets longer hair and a simpler costume. Taylor experiments with different compositions before settling on the final concept, in which a standing girl is surrounded by a skirt made of ribbons and Luna moths. A photograph Taylor took in Spain becomes a part of the backdrop. Unsatisfied with the color scheme of Figure II, Taylor gives the image a grayscale adjustment layer to help her settle on a new scheme.

FIGURE 1

FIGURE 2

FIGURE 3

FIGURE 4

FIGURE 5

FIGURE 6

FIGURE 7

FIGURE 8

FIGURE 9

FIGURE 10

FIGURE 11

FIGURE 12

FIGURE 13

FIGURE 14

FIGURE 15

Man with too much time

MAN WITH TOO MUCH TIME BEGINS with an undated tintype. First, the tintype is trimmed into a square format and cleaned of dust spots and tears; then Taylor adds color. Taylor photographs paper airplanes made by Uelsmann and adds them along with a wastebasket created with painting tools in Photoshop. A background layer of clouds, photographed by Taylor in Gainesville, enhances the new backdrop in the final image.

FIGURE 1

FIGURE 2

FIGURE 3

FIGURE 4

FIGURE 5

FIGURE 6

FIGURE 7

Surrounded

SURROUNDED BEGINS WITH a photograph, probably dating to the early twentieth century. The photograph is scanned and retouched, then Taylor adjusts the global tonal levels using Photoshop curves. Taylor gives color to skin and clothing, adds mice and shadows, and experiments with a spotlight effect created on an adjustment layer with a mask. In Figure 6, Taylor auditions (and later abandons) a bold backdrop and baseboard. In the final image, the figure is placed in a landscape made from photos Taylor took of grass in her backyard and trees on the horizon.

FIGURE 1

FIGURE 2

FIGURE 3

FIGURE 4

FIGURE 5

FIGURE 6

FIGURE 7

Girl with a bee dress

GIRL WITH A BEE DRESS BEGINS with a photograph Taylor took of herself, to which she added a mottled texture for an aged quality. Next, she adds the head of a girl, taken from a nineteenth century photograph. Taylor scans six of the carpenter bees that collect in the windowsills of her studio into her computer. She copies and transforms them, creating the illusion of a dress-shaped swarm. A background photograph taken in an Irish bog is added. Final steps involve considering a necklace, replacing the flower, and adjusting the colors.

FIGURE 1

FIGURE 2

FIGURE 3

FIGURE 4

FIGURE 5

FIGURE 6

FIGURE 7

{ Man who loves fish, 2003. }

{ Almost winners, 2004. }

{ Good girls, 2003. }

{ Waiting room, 2002. }

{ Cloud sisters, 2001. }

{ Optimist's suit, 2003. }

"Let us resolve, therefore: the Marvellous is always beautiful,

everything marvellous is beautiful.

Nothing but the Marvellous is beautiful."

—from Le Manifeste du Surréalisme,

André Breton, 1924.

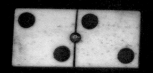

CHAPTER FOUR

Nothing but the Marvelous

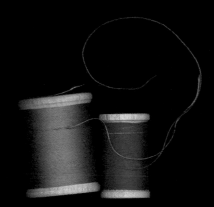

*I*s Taylor's work surrealist? It's one of the first words used to describe her images of impossible situations, lit by impossible light, and populated by an improbable cast of animal-human hybrids, masked or disfigured faces, and objects floating in space. Like the Surrealists' work, Taylor's pictures mean to trigger the subconscious, to free viewers from the constraints of the rational world so that, as Taylor describes it, they experience "a convergence of factual memory and fictional daydream." Eighty-one years ago, in his *First Surrealist Manifesto*, the French artist André Breton wrote that Surrealists believed "in the omnipotence of the dream, and in the disinterested play of thought." For Taylor, the dream isn't omnipotent, but it's a beginning. Photoshop, and the long process of experimenting, adding and taking away layers, are the means by which that "disinterested play of thought" takes place. In front of her computer, Taylor watches her images grow in directions she couldn't have predicted. Accidents give birth to new ideas; one added element suggests another. It's not unlike a digital analog for the free association exercises that the twentieth century European Surrealists practiced.

{ One and a half sisters, 2003. }

But the word "surrealist" more often refers to Taylor's completed images than to her process. Her iconography, based as it often is in dreams and recollections of childhood and fantasy, can be strikingly surrealistic. Take the eggs in Taylor's *Small possibility*, *Messenger*, or *One and a half sisters*, for example. In 1933, the Belgian surrealist René Magritte completed *Elective Affinities,* in which a caged egg hangs from a sturdy wooden frame. It may be a reference to Breton's *Manifesto*: "Boundaries have been assigned even to experience. It revolves in a cage from which release is becoming increasingly difficult." If, in Magritte's image, raw experience is represented in the form of an egg, what are we to make of Taylor's *One and a half sisters*? Here, the egg is cradled in the hands of a blindfolded woman. Next to her, her

"half" sister, who holds a living bird in her lap, is fading away. In this image, as in Magritte's, the egg is shorthand for unrealized potential, as threatening as a grenade or as auspicious as a wrapped gift.

In Taylor's images, as in Breton's *Manifesto* and Magritte's painting, the world is split in two: there are the "factual objects" of our everyday lives—the suitcase, the umbrella, the egg, the house—and then there is the situation into which it's been plunged, the "fictional daydream." An egg in a dream is a very different thing from an egg in real life. One must shed the expectations of real life before entering, as Mark Sloan describes it, Taylor's "realm of the purely imaginary."

Many of Taylor's images—*One and half sisters* is only one example—are populated with human beings in varying stages of existence: fading in and out of being, like ghosts or memories, or fragmented, with detached or missing heads. Taylor says these figures may represent "people who just can't deal with reality," or who've "lost their heads." On one level, it's a vision of insanity; on another, it's a reference to dreams, where we trade in reality and our conscious minds for a surreal, dream-state logic. Again, there's a clear parallel in surrealist thinking. In 1965, Magritte painted *The Blank Signature*, depicting a man riding through the woods. The picture is an optical puzzle: the horse and rider are cut vertically into disappearing slices by the trees they pass through. They're both there and not there, defying the laws of physics and everyday logic. Taylor doesn't describe her own *Strange beast* (page 55) in surrealist terms, but the resemblance between the two images is clear.

Like the Surrealists, Taylor returns time and again to the imagery and associations of her childhood. Here, imagination is paramount, unburdened by the banal errand-running (alluded to in *Pretty busy today* (page 153) and the busywork of adulthood. In Taylor's *Dreamer* (page 56), for example, a child's dreams are as light as clouds. Other images might have been plucked from the pages of fairy tales, as in *Distracted cats* (page 106) or *Man pretending to be a rabbit* (page 31). "Children set off each day without a worry in the world," wrote Breton. "Everything is near at hand, the worst material conditions are excellent. The woods are black or white, one will never sleep." This is the netherworld of Taylor's child protagonists. The woods in *Moth dancer*, for example, (page 5) are dark, but the girl is fearless

and dances on. Taylor's children live in a dangerous world, but they're unconcerned. They rarely sleep, and when they do, as in *Dreamer*, their dreams are a passport to magic. They're almost heroic, these children of Taylor's, and at least part of their appeal must be that they don't yet know their limits, as in the flight-envying *Butterfly jumper* (page 125).

The genre of Surrealism refers to an enormous scope of artists and images (not to mention literature, film, and sculpture), only some of which bears any relation to Taylor's work. Taylor's closest analog in surrealist art would be to the earlier, dreamier works—what Joseph Cornell called the "Max Ernst white magic side" of surrealism—less than to the later, darker, and more sexual works. There are traces of this "dark magic" in Taylor's work: take the menacing leer of *Just looking* (page 54), for instance. But Taylor's images, as unsettling as they may be, lack the sexual violence of, say, Hans Bellmer's *Doll* series, in which women's body parts are thrown together into grotesque anatomical collages. In Taylor's images, the violence is never specific, and it's rarely sexual. It's the darkness of a child's nightmare or a Grimm's fairytale: Hansel and Gretel being fattened up for the wicked witch of the forest.

Taylor's images are often funny, but they don't pull pranks the way the Dadaists, as in Duchamp's *L.H.O.O.Q.* or *Fountain*, did. Taylor makes jokes by providing a glimpse into a scenario that is absurd—you're in on it just by virtue of looking at the picture. There's no hidden puzzle behind *The bachelorette*, for example, in which a prim older woman with an elaborate lace collar and brooch is festooned with bunny ears and a yellow daisy. The

{ Distracted cats, 2003. }

{ The bachelorette, 2003. }

Messenger, 1999.

The Hotel Eden,
Joseph Cornell, 1945.

Art © The Joseph and
Robert Cornell Memorial
Foundation/Licensed
by VAGA, New York, NY.

juxtaposition *is* the joke. And as often as not, in Taylor's images, the joke is just the beginning: We laugh at the bachelorette, until the note of pathos starts peeking through. She's not pleased to be sitting there, but her scratched halo suggests she doesn't really have a choice. Meanwhile, the white masks of her suitors begin to appear a bit ominous. Along the way, the woman has been transformed from caricature into character, and Taylor's sympathies have revealed themselves. In this woman's time, after all, there was no glamour in being a bachelorette, and the rituals of courtship must have seemed tedious and embarrassing. It's not the kind of story that would have interested the surrealists.

Except, maybe, Cornell. From the 1930s through the 1960s, Cornell built intimate worlds in boxes, drawing from his collection of small treasures picked up on expeditions to Manhattan and squirreled away in the studio of a house he shared with his mother and brother on Utopia Parkway, in Queens. Cornell's work, like Taylor's, was solitary, personal, and often enigmatic. He tended to specific, almost obsessively revisited interests, like film stars, astronomy, and the ballet. He treated the simplest objects—a cork, a cheap necklace, a scrap of paper—like treasures, sanctified for some innate quality initially only apparent to himself. (Perhaps Taylor experienced a similar pleasure admiring the "perfect" helicopter of her childhood Playskool airport.) The mementos and scraps of Cornell's foraging weren't just props, they were the instigation of the whole artistic process. If eBay can be seen as the modern equivalent of those 1950s Manhattan junk shops, these two artists' processes start looking similar.

The Language of Objects

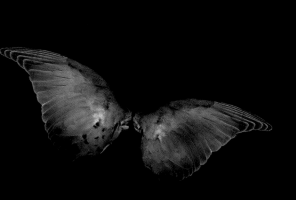

MOST PEOPLE, AT ONE POINT OR ANOTHER, DREAM OF FLIGHT, which may be why images of birds were so potent to surrealist artists like Cornell, Magritte, Salvador Dalí, and Max Ernst, whose childhood alter-ego was a bird-man named Loplop. Many of Cornell's boxes contained images of birds, actual stuffed birds, or parts of birds. In Cornell's *The Hotel Eden*, a parrot appears trapped in a French hotel, its gaze directed to what might be a window above. Birds mean flight and flight means freedom from constraint, the central objective of the Surrealist project. For Cornell, often just a single feather was enough to connote that stark contrast between land-bound humans and the limitlessness of a bird in flight.

Taylor has had flying dreams since childhood. In her nightmares, flight offers an escape from harm; in other dreams, it symbolizes a release from the daily concerns of life. The wings sprouting from the back of a nineteenth century woman's dress in *Turning* add another layer to this idea. *Turning* suggests freedom from strict codes of morality, particularly those moral codes which confined nineteenth century women.

{ Turning, 2001. }

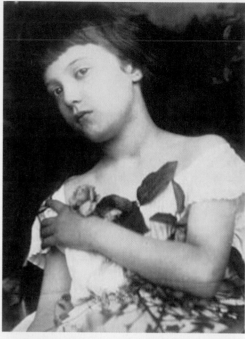

As Trudy Wilner Stack points out in Chapter Two, this fascination with birds and other fauna has a distinctly Victorian flavor. Taylor finds butterflies, bees, bones, and feathers in her own garden, and carries them inside to her study, where she places them on the flatbed scanner and records their images for later use. One hundred years ago, such collecting and cataloging was a consuming passion for amateur naturalists inspired by Charles Darwin's newly published *Origin of Species* and by the exotic artifacts being transported back from the New World. Victorian naturalists collected specimens under bell jars or in glass cases, and recorded the minutia of their markings and behaviors in the etchings Taylor buys today on eBay (page 67).

This sensitivity to both the natural world and to objects in general has marked Taylor's work all along. She is a contemporary version, as Wilner Stack suggests, of those Victorians "who pressed flowers and put them in their diaries and wrote about a walk in the woods and a letter they received from someone and different impacts of the shades of the color blue."

Nineteenth century encyclopedias, natural history catalogs, and such things were typically men's work. Women of that era were more likely to make albums, thick volumes of leather and cardboard into which they pressed leaves, photographs, and other mementos. Like quilting and embroidery, album-making gave women an outlet for their creative energies, and an opportunity to impress themselves upon the world with objects that would outlive them. Albums were also a venue for educated women whose social status precluded them from leaving the house for work or adventure. The album makers, like the women in Taylor's tintypes and ambrotypes, have long since become anonymous.

The Victorian photographer Julia Margaret Cameron is one notable exception. A Calcutta-born member of the poet Alfred Lord Tennyson's artistic circle, Cameron photographed her friends and family dressed up as historical and biblical figures or in idealized rural settings. Like Taylor's images, Cameron's work reveals an acute sensitivity to the natural world, and a warm, dreamlike ambience.

A connection may also be drawn to a much more recent American photographer, Ralph Eugene Meatyard, whose 1974 book *The Family Album of Lucybelle Crater*, depicted friends and family members posing with comically gruesome dimestore masks. Their faces obscured, the figures in Meatyard's fictional family album are transformed into universal characters, each bearing the same name, Lucybelle Crater. Meatyard, an optician by trade, was also a Zen Buddhist, and his masks suggest the difficulty of seeing through the superficial appearances of human beings into a universal, true self.

Taylor's images of human figures in animal masks or, again, with missing or removed heads, often have a similar effect: Their anonymity makes them universal; we can see in them whatever we want to.

Ambrose Bierce, the journalist and writer after whom Meatyard named a series of his photographs, defined "romance" in his *Devil's Dictionary* as "fiction that owes no allegiance to the God of Things as They Are." In the novel, Bierce wrote, "the writers thought is tethered to probability, as a domestic horse to the hitching post, but in romance, it ranges free will over the entire region of the imagination—free, lawless, immune to bit and rein."

If anything, this "romantic" aspect is the thread that runs through Cameron's, Meatyard's, and Taylor's work. Composed of everyday figures, recognizable humans and objects, these images have an overall effect that is fantastic, unreal, untethered to probability and, by Bierce's logic, truest to human imagination.

⁓

ANONYMITY IS CENTRAL to the success of that romance. These figures aren't just untethered to reality, they've become estranged from the circumstances of their actual lives. Who was that woman with the stiff lace collar we see in *The bachelorette*? How did she wish us to think of her? Was her photograph given as a gift, and if so, to whom? How did an object once so meaningful come to be so anonymous and generic?

We see some of the same questions in Taylor's photographs from her undergraduate days. New Haven, through Taylor's lens, is a ghost town:

The landscape near
Gainesville, Florida.

The tilting bird houses, built and then neglected, the oil slick in the driveway (page 10), the recently plowed passageway in front of the house. These traces of human behavior seem to fascinate Taylor in much the same way as do the dolls and tintypes of her contemporary collections. They allude to an individual, specific person who has since moved out of the frame of the picture. In Taylor's hands, the toys and scraps of paper and old photographs are artifacts, cast-offs from a forgotten life. Who played with those die-cast dollhouse chairs until the paint wore thin at the corners? Which class so bored Taylor's grandmother that she covered her schoolbook with doodles? The stuff we leave behind makes fertile ground for mystery and creation.

Peter Bunnell describes this recreation, or reinvention, as a feminist project and, in a sense it is. If not for their recasting at Taylor's computer,

all those Victorian women might have remained anonymous forever. Taylor rescues them from the flea market scrap heap and turns them into the central characters of dramas that, as Wilner Stack observes, have no obvious place in time. Formerly locked in their one-of-a-kind glass negatives, these women are freed from history, digitized, printed, bought and sold, and looked at until our own technology, like their own, becomes obsolete. Those women aren't immortal, but they're closer to it.

Of course, Taylor works with images of men, too, though less often. Perhaps that's simply because, to Taylor, the woman is the default protagonist of these fantasy worlds, just as Taylor stars in her own dreams. These are, after all, at least semi-autobiographical images, and it follows that Taylor

Pages from a grade school text book or "reader" that belonged to Maggie Taylor's grandmother.

would chose characters that remind her, in some rudimentary way, of herself. And often, the resemblance isn't just coincidental; Taylor occasionally appears in her own work. In *Mood lifter*, a head is held aloft by the decapitated figure of Taylor herself, cropped from a photograph taken with a self-timer in the artist's Gainesville backyard.

Gainesville makes a good backdrop for Taylor's stories. The landscape is lush and unremittingly flat. In some places it's thick and jungly, full of mosquitoes, and overwhelmingly fertile. In others, the vegetation is low, and the skyline horizontal for miles. Taylor often drives to Payne's Prairie, an expansive swamp just outside of town, to take photographs which make up the background in images like *Woman with swan*, *The bachelorette*, and others.

As Uelsmann observes, the landscape around Gainesville is "intricately layered. ... There's a reality beneath the surface reality that is waiting to be discovered." Indeed, it's tempting to start fictionalizing this landscape, which seems so ripe

with metaphor and hidden meaning. Payne's Prairie looks innocuous from a distance, but you wouldn't want to swim there. Flushed with the water from the aquifer below, the prairie is home to one of the world's largest concentrations of alligators, along with a thriving community of water moccasins. Florida, like California, is a place where dreams and reality collide. Mythologized by Hollywood as a place of palm trees and leisure, Florida often delivers a different reality entirely, as the strip of seedy motels on Gainesville's Route 441 suggests. Gainesville itself is far from the beachy towns of Ft.

Who played with those die-cast dollhouse chairs until the paint wore thin at the corners? Which class so bored Taylor's grandmother that she doodled all over her schoolbook?

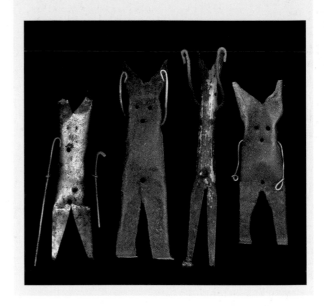

Lauderdale and Long Beach, but it too is a city of contrasts: a liberal, artistic university community surrounded by Bible Belt.

Southern gothic (page 39) is Taylor's most explicit mention of the landscape where she lives. In it, English ivy threatens to smother the girl at the center of the frame, who maintains a placid expression while tearing herself in two. The juxtaposition is of calm versus violence, order versus the chaotic, overwhelming force of nature.

Photographer Sally Mann, often cited as an example of a Southern aesthetic in contemporary photography, uses her own misty, mossy landscape to a similarly moody effect. But in Mann's images, the human figures are part of the landscape, organically connected to it; in Taylor's they tend to defy it. Taylor is fascinated by the South, but unlike Mann, she's a transplant, and it's her own inner, subliminal world that her images depict.

Totems and Magic

OFTENTIMES, TAYLOR'S WORLD involves an element of mysticism, or references to ritual or alchemic processes, as in *The scientist* (page 139), or *The alchemists*. That same interest runs through Taylor and Uelsmann's art collection, which emphasizes ritual objects from Brazil, Africa, and Cuba, and American Indian groups. Taylor has said that she's drawn to the "no-man's-land" of the religious imagination, where "people turn into animals, or fly." In Chapter Three, Taylor reminds herself to make an image based on a Brazilian *ex voto* figure with a long, exaggerated scar. At the time, it was just one such image she was mulling over. "I'd like to make a person with a hole in the shape of their totemic animal in their body," Taylor said one day, "like a bird-shaped hole burned through a body." In some ways, this could be described as a contemporary branch of the surrealist project. These totems of religious belief, says Taylor, are "the physical imagery that comes out of subconscious, ritualistic, and mystical origins."

The Surrealists also loved outsider art, generally

{ The alchemists, 2001. }

Strange case, 2002.

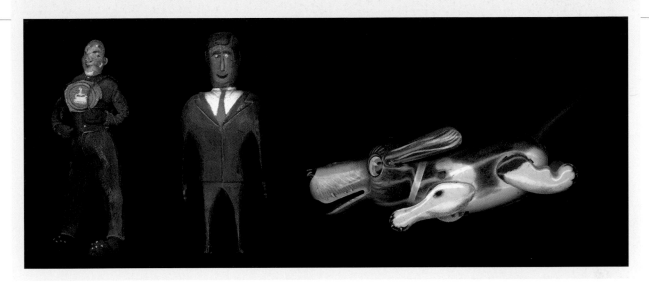

Objects from Taylor and
Uelsmann's collection.

defined as art made by artists who work completely
outside of the art world, and whose work, at least in
theory, communicates only one vision and frame of
reference, the artist's own. Art Brut, or raw art, the
art of the insane, became popular around the time of
Freud's studies of the subconscious. Since the insane
existed outside of all social convention, their art,
reasoned the Surrealists, must come directly from
the unschooled self, and contain precisely that inno-
cent, untarnished reality they'd been looking for.

Taylor and Uelsmann's collection contains
many pieces of outsider art and Art Brut. Taylor
loves the personal quality of these objects, the nar-
ratives implicit in them, and the hand-touched
quality, the craft.

For an artist working with the latest digital
tools, Taylor's artistic impulses are actually quite
traditional. Much is made of her medium and of
the modern tools she uses to make her images.
It's a conversation Taylor is always willing to have;
her love of objects extends, perhaps, to a general
fondness for the latest technologies and how they
can help her better realize her ideas. But as novel as
her tools may be, Taylor's medium is just that. Her
work rarely, if ever, seems to reflect on the tools
used to make it, nor provide commentary on the
state of art, or where it's going. Taylor uses whatever technology seems best for the job. Right now,
that's Photoshop and an Epson scanner. One day,
Taylor muses, she might like to explore filmmaking,
or sculpture.

Taylor's medium may change, but it's likely
she'll continue to create images which work beneath
the skin, jarring the viewer out of her everyday surroundings and throwing out a line to some other,
stranger, plane. To borrow another term from
Breton, Taylor's work celebrates the marvelous, in
all its darkness and mystery.

{ Party girl, 2002. }

{ Woman with bees, 2001. }

{ Subject to change, 2004. }

{ Abdullah's prayer, 2003. }

{ Man in his own world, 2004. }

{ Butterfly jumper, 2002. }

"If you asked me about the computer 15 years ago,

I could never have envisioned using one for my work

Now it absolutely makes sense to me as a form of weaving together

all of my objects and interests. And thank goodness

I took typing in seventh grade."

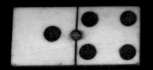

CHAPTER FIVE

Taylor on Taylor

WHEN I FIRST BROACHED THE IDEA with Taylor of a chapter in which she would speak specifically about her own work, she was less than enthusiastic. "Wouldn't that be boring?" She showed me a magazine article in which the writer had, more or less, done the same thing, pairing Taylor's images with bits of text in which she was asked to describe each image, where it came from, how she made it. And she was right: it was boring. Knowing, for example, that *Birthday girl* was inspired by a family argument in Taylor's childhood that culminated in her mother throwing a cake at Taylor's sister didn't make the image any more interesting to look at. In fact, it made it less interesting: Described so tidily, *Birthday girl* became a puzzle, and an easily solved one, at that. The family story didn't only take some of the mystery out of *Birthday girl*, it shortchanged it, by distilling the image to only a few of its elements, and preventing the viewer from responding to it personally. When I look at that image, I see all the forced gaiety of a birthday party, how much we sometimes strain to celebrate, and how easily the

{ Late, 2000. }

{ Surrounded, 2004. }

bubble is burst. Coming up with my own explanation is half the pleasure of looking at a Maggie
Taylor image.

Taylor describes the difference between illustration and her work this way: "In most commercial
illustration pieces," she says, "you can tell what the
person was told to communicate and whether they
have succeeded." Taylor's work cannot be so easily
deciphered. Though her images are representational, there is always an element that "goes beyond"
the representational or iconographic, some part
of an image that speaks to the viewer on emotional
terms, encourages her to compose her own story
about what's happening in the frame. The point of
these images, Taylor suggests, is to fire up the movie
projectors we all carry around in our own minds.

Taylor is constantly writing stories in her
mind (blame it on all that television she watched
as a child). She is a lover of all things narrative
and tends to respond to the world and to her own
thoughts as if she were watching them on a big
screen: "Now that would make a great movie!"
Taylor often says upon waking up from a dream.

If Taylor were a different kind of artist, she'd
publish a manifesto and explain to us how each
image fits into a grand plan of art and philosophy,
but that's not her way. For better or for worse, she
leaves the interpreting to us. This chapter, therefore, contains no explanations or keys to Taylor's
images. Rather it's a conversation around them,
between me, Taylor, and the strange universe her
images depict.

MANY OF YOUR IMAGES REMIND ME **of dreams, or of that pre-sleep state, where the line between what's imagined and what's real becomes fuzzy, and the mind runs free. Two I think of in particular are** *Moth dancer* **and** *Surrounded*. **Both remind me of dreams I had when I was a child, where I was on the verge of being attacked by monsters or some other terrifying but abstract threat. It's like being afraid of the dark—you aren't sure exactly what you're scared of, you're just scared. What are your dreams like?**

> I don't particularly remember being scared a lot as a kid. But I have always had a lot of nightmares. I don't know why, I just do. I had two last night. I dream about burglars, robbers, and murderers— and sometimes noises in the night can trigger the dreams. This has happened ever since I was a child.

In general, I have vivid, very detailed dreams, and I usually remember them pretty well. Sometimes, I do forget them, but then the next night, just at the moment that I put my head down on the pillow, the dream comes back to me. It's brief, and I don't reenact the whole dream, but as I lie down, I'll think "Oh my gosh, there was that dream about the Icelandic fisherman with the big block of ice," or something like that. It is a flashback to the previous night, not unlike the opening segment of a TV show where they remind you of what happened on the previous episode.

What else do you dream about?

> I have a lot of dreams about flying that involve butterfly wings, or bird wings attached to me. Sometimes these evolve out of a scary dream as a means of escape, enabling me to fly into the treetops. I have a strong connection to images of flight and to the idea that a winged creature can be positive or hopeful.

I also have dreams where I'm not being chased but I realize that I can fly and that no one else can. I have to fly at night when people aren't watching, because I don't want to be too obvious about it. So I take off from the roof at night and fly all over the place.

In these dreams, is flying a joyful, liberating feeling?

> Definitely. And every once in awhile, people see me flying, and I must explain to them why I have this skill. I encourage them to help keep it a secret.

Many of your images depict people or animals in flight. Do your images draw from your dreams?

> At times when I wake up in the morning I write

{ Night garden, 2000. }

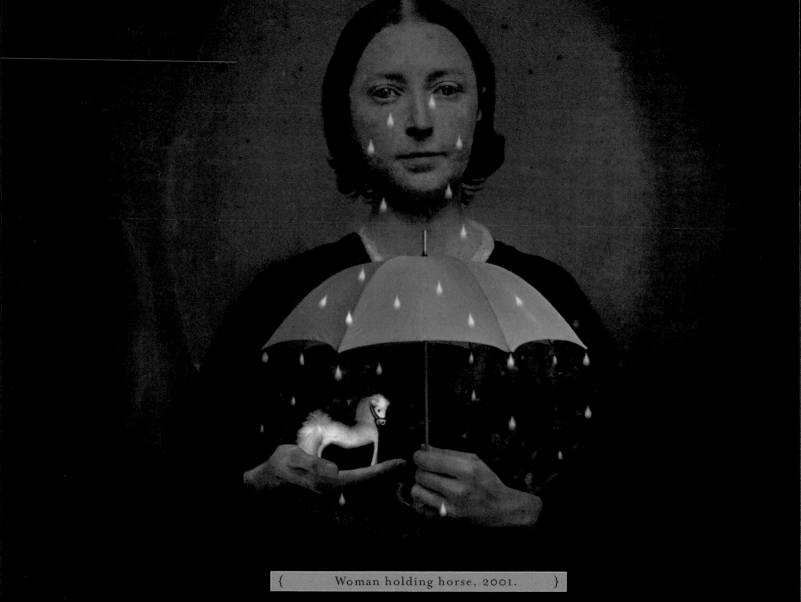

{ Woman holding horse, 2001. }

my dreams in a bedside notebook. It might be just a few sentences or a diagram; sometimes it is a complete story. Every once in a while a dream migrates from this notebook to the computer in the form of an image. But the images rarely reflect the dream accurately. Somehow "dream logic" and "image logic" operate differently. If I go to the computer and end up with a really literal interpretation of something that occurred to me in a dream, I often feel that the mystery has vanished; the more I work on it, the less I like it. Sometimes I'll have a dream about a strange character maybe a human-animal hybrid of some sort—and it will end up in an image, but rarely is it that direct. An image from a dream sometimes leads to something else entirely. The dream is just something I try to preserve as a point of departure for future images.

Can you give an example?
> Well, *Surrounded*, the image of the dancing girl surrounded by a circle of mice, was based on a recurring dream. In this dream, I was surrounded by rodents in a small room. But they weren't pleasant little mice, they were large rats gnashing their teeth. And I wasn't a dancer in the dream. As it happened, a friend alerted me to this image of the young ballerina on eBay. Just after I "won" it, and scanned it to begin retouching it, I had another one of these dreams about the rats. So chance played a part in the image coming together, as it often does.

Why did the image change from being frightening into this more positive, happier image?
> I don't know, really. I guess visually it made more sense when the rodents were smaller and in a more orderly arrangement. The ballerina has an air of calmness and elegance about her. The whole room full of rats … well, I might do something with that someday in another image.

Did you ever think of doing dream analysis, or reading about what these dreams might mean?
> I've read a little bit, but I prefer to believe that people can't fully explain dreams. I don't think there is a one-to-one correlation between elements

Rabbit test, 2003.

in our dreams and an explanation of reality. The dreamlike sensibility is what appeals to me, and I hope to convey it through the images.

Sure, dreams mean different things to different people. On the other hand, a lot of the objects you include in your images are very clearly symbolic, in a universal, archetypal way—the eggs, for instance.

> Yes, there's definitely something about the collective unconscious, a collective pool of imagery that many people relate to in one way or another. Wings, butterflies, certain animals that conjure up specific emotions or ideas.

Is that the language that we should use to decode or understand your work?

> In some sense, my images function in this more predictable way, with elements that can be decoded. But then I hope that they get around, or go beyond the predictable or universal. An archetypal reference might be a doorway through which you enter one of the images, but then further explanation or exploration is required (or at least encouraged). In this way I hope they become more personal and more poetic.

You have always been a big fan of television. Do your dreams ever feel TV-like, or does TV ever feel dreamlike to you?

> I have had the dream-within-a-dream experience at times, when a dream is interrupted by someone saying "Maggie, this would really make a great TV show!" Or I'll wake up from a particularly elaborate dream and say to myself, "This would be the best screenplay in the world! I've got to write it down!" Usually, when I think about these dreams later, they defy logic and would not make sense to anyone else. But at the time, they often feel like the kinds of stories you'd see on TV.

Growing up, what were your favorite television shows?

> I was a real *Star Trek* junkie. I have not watched the newer series, but I used to know the original ones by heart. I read every *Star Trek* book, watched every episode probably ten times.

I stopped watching TV for a little while when I went to high school. There was only one TV in the dorm, and it didn't have good reception. The only thing we watched was *Saturday Night Live*. But then later, I got my own TV and had it in my dorm room in college, and I was back in business. I watched *Dynasty, All My Children*, various game shows. It was really a mindless escape from all my reading and course work.

Do you think all that television shows up anywhere in your work?

> On TV news and close-ups in many shows, a large portion of what you see is the head and shoulders shot—the "talking head" centered in the screen. In my images, I actually try to come up with alterations and strategies to get away from it, but I seem to gravitate towards that kind of composition. Of course it also has a lot to do with the old portraits I scan. Often they're just that simple head-and-shoulders pose; sometimes they start at the waist.

Donald Roller Wilson, 2004.

I frequently try to add on to them to move away from the television composition.

Do the recurring characters in your images take part in plots?
> No, right now there are not plots that connect the individual images. But as time goes on, I can't say what might happen. I have a tendency to re-use certain characters (particularly animals) that I like. The bees, the purple plastic cow named Red Larry, and some of the fish have migrated into more than one image. At some point, perhaps, the people

themselves will start to jump from image to image. But for right now, I think of the people in the images as if they are caught mid-story.

The luminous and colorful paintings of Donald Roller Wilson come to mind when I think of art with a plot. In his paintings, chimpanzees, dogs and cats in human dress each tell a story, and the story is interwoven from image to image. Over time, he's developed a cast of characters in his parallel universe and uses text on the image and on the frames to help clarify the plot.

{ The scientist, 2004. }

Wilson's process is so different from yours. He maps out his paintings very early on, which means he has to know from the beginning what he wants them to look like. You seem to spend a lot of time in front of the computer experimenting. Does chance play a role in how your images turn out?

> Yes, definitely. Everyday events, trips I take and things I see play a role all the time. Today I needed a landscape for the background of an image, so I started experimenting with different photographs I'd taken on a recent trip. Depending on where I have been recently, different sorts of landscapes are immediately at hand in my computer. I picked four or five likely images with trees on the horizon and opened them all up. I put one landscape into the new image and then a second one on top. I meant to turn them on and off one at a time to decide which I preferred, but by mistake, I actually changed the transparency of the top one, and realized that the two landscapes together had an interesting layered effect that looked like hills in fog. It's not something I could have planned out ahead of time; it was a gift of chance.

Can you think of an image where the final product surprised you because of how different it was than what you'd imagined initially?

> That's the case with almost all of my images, and for me this is a good thing. When I try to force myself to stick to the initial idea, the image can start to seem very forced and much less interesting to work on. One example is *Rabbit test*, which started out with a person in the middle of the image, and the rabbit as just a small element. While making adjustments and reworking it and becoming increasingly disillusioned with the way the person looked, I started reconsidering the rabbit as the main subject. The coffee was introduced after many days of working with the rabbit, as an element he could interact with. Sometimes I rummage through all the drawers in my study and see what I can find that might work in a particular circumstance. For the rabbit, I think I tried three or four different things and finally decided on the very domestic-looking cup and saucer.

Then what do you make of that image? Is it just a random collection of objects or figures that work well together?

> I don't think it's random. It could be an echo of something I've recently read, or seen in a film. Those things have a way of percolating through to the images, though not necessarily at a conscious level. The images have to make some sense to me not only visually, but literally, for me to be happy with them. There has to be some story in my mind about why the rabbit is wearing the blindfold, and why the coffee cup is there and why it's steaming. There has to be a strange kind of logic to it.

Can you tell me what the story is in *Rabbit test* or would that ruin it?

> I don't think I know anymore, and if I did, I would be reluctant to share it. Sometimes it's better not to know. For me, the stories are fleeting and malleable things. They are very delicate. At the time I'm working on the image, the story makes sense. When I am finished and save the image, I can come

{ Buffalo with wings, 2002. }

{ Seven sisters, 1998. }

back to it months later and see it in a different light. Sometimes I still have the story at that point; sometimes the story may have transformed into something else. I like to think that people who look at my images will come up with their own stories.

I think that the folk art Jerry and I like works in a similar way; inviting the viewer to engage in a kind of dialog or daydream. I imagine that when someone is carving a figure, working for many hours on something, they have stories running through their heads, too. They're thinking about a particular person, a particular dog or Great Aunt Hilda's illness. Then, a hundred years later, if you or I find that object at a flea market or an antique store, even if we have no idea who made it or why, that doesn't matter. The object itself is hinting at a story and has the ability to transport us to another time and place.

What other kinds of art do you like?
> When I'm traveling and get the chance to visit a museum or a gallery, I like to see everything from Gothic religious paintings to conceptual sculpture. I never know when something will cause me to reconsider my own work. Sometimes in the most surprising places I find something that sparks an idea for a new image. But I would have to admit that I'm much more drawn to narrative, emotionally based art than to more intellectual, minimalist art. I love images that stay with me for a long time—things that I want to visit again and again.

In addition to folk painting and sculpture, I love Joseph Cornell's boxes with his unexpected but ordinary objects. They invite an almost dreamlike

meditation for me. Since I am working with very simple portraits as my initial images, I find it very intriguing to see medieval and Renaissance portraits, for example, Hans Holbein's work. The very plain backgrounds in saturated colors, along with the black clothing and symbolic objects the people are holding, attract me. Some of the images are almost photographic. There is also a strange glow which reminds me of the light created by the scanner—a slightly eerie, very flat look. The colors are super-saturated and lush and thick.

Tell me about the tintypes and ambrotypes you use. What do you look for in them? What sort of people and poses are you attracted to?
> I have gone through phases of seeking and responding to different things in these nineteenth century images. At first I used mostly images of women, sometimes combining them with parts of toys or having them interact with toys and other small objects. I was a bit reluctant to use images of children initially, as they seemed almost too precious, too cute. But then my mother gave me two really clear tintypes of nearly identical boys in our own family, and after working with them, I went through a time when I sought out more images of children. In about 2001, I realized that I had not made as many images of men, so I made an effort to correct that. The condition of the tintypes is not that important to me. Not only is it relatively easy to correct in Photoshop, but in fact, cracks and fading can be visually interesting.

I've recently found some occupational tintypes that show people in their work uniforms, or doing

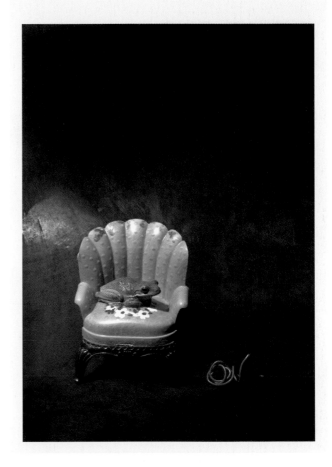

something related to their jobs. There is one of a man, I guess he's a scientist, posing in a lab coat with his beakers, demonstrating a pouring action. I have always had a fascination with scientific experiments. Although I was really good at math in school, I somehow never took any science classes. Well, I took one class: chemistry. But the only thing I remember was an experiment involving testing shampoos to find the one with the best pH for your hair, so I don' t think it was a "true" science class. I had been told that in biology you would have to dissect a frog, so I was careful to avoid that class. But now I seem to collect all kinds of scientific beakers, tubes, eyedroppers, and pieces of electronics and need to find a use for them.

Nowadays, photographs seem so unimportant and disposable. We take so many—especially with digital cameras—and only print a small percentage of them. In the nineteenth century it was very much the opposite. People may have been photographed only once or twice in their lifetimes, and it was a very special occasion, perhaps a wedding or engagement. It was also a pretty uncomfortable procedure. Exposures usually were long, so people could not have very fleeting expressions like smiles. They would have to keep their eyes open as much as possible, and hold still. That's why you see a lot of them holding on to a chair or leaning on a table or railing; some even have an actual stand behind them. In both *Man with too much time* and *Moth dancer* there was a metal brace or stand behind the person,

and I debated whether or not to remove it. In the end I decided that the stand was not an essential part of the image, so for simplicity's sake, I retouched it.

Before you started using the tintypes and ambrotypes—and especially before you were introduced to Photoshop—you worked with a lot of family artifacts: photos, toys, even pieces

of dialogue or stories you remembered from childhood. It's as if you've rescued these fragments and—in the process of arranging and photographing them—turned them from personal objects into iconic ones. It seems to me that this is where we're starting to see your great interest in objects, and in collecting. Also, there is a stage-like or diorama quality to them that continues through much of your later work.

> I can remember obsessively sitting for hours and hours when I was a kid, sometimes alone, sometimes with my sister or a girlfriend from the neighborhood, and we would divvy up a pile of toys and blocks and each build a house. We were playing architects and it was a wonderful feeling to create something new and unexpected each time. When I work on my images, it's a little bit of this same feeling.

Back then I had certain collections started. I collected pill boxes and pigs; my sister collected frogs. I still have most of these things and it seemed natural to try to incorporate them into my work at some point. During my first year as a graduate photography student, I was struggling to find a way to make my work more personally relevant—trying to look inward rather than outward. Using some of these bits and pieces I had saved since childhood seemed like a beginning. This was how I started to work on my

still-life photographs, which also included childlike drawings and scraps of paper with text.

At about the same time, I started going to flea markets (a popular North Florida activity, along with yard sales) and looking around at other people's junk. I realized that while my family objects have a certain meaning to me, there might be other, more interesting objects out there. In fact there were toys and broken bits of things many decades older than what I had been working with from my own 1960s plastic-era childhood. The authenticity, sense of wear and tear, and layers of dirt and rust spoke to me.

What are the qualities you look for in an object or a photograph?

> There are some objects that I come across—for example, a really beat-up, wonderful old leather doll with one leg missing from the knee down, and right away I know that this is something I could use in an image. Other times, I find something that I think is really fascinating, but it ends up sitting in the drawer for years before I can use it. I have an old plastic doll that must have melted in a fire or in someone's hot Southern attic, and I love it, but can't find a way to use it yet.

I look for things that have a sense of graceful wear, things that can communicate through layers of paint or dirt. So instead of a toy car, it might be an old rusted piece of a toy car—something that's been used and left outside and fallen apart.

Something that's been loved to death?

> Or neglected. Sometimes it's been too well loved

{ Woman who loves fish, 2003. }

{ Dog with stick, 2002. }

and used over and over, or sometimes it's been neglected.

Not all of your images have a suggestion of something ominous about them, but many of them do. I've described this quality elsewhere as the scariness of a child's nightmare. In other cases, I wouldn't know how to characterize it, other than to say it's something about the light, or the way the frame closes in around the central figure, like in *Fighting man,* **for example. And then, of course, there are all the blurred or missing heads…**

> I think I have a habit of making images that fall on either side of an emotional spectrum. There are very pleasant, bucolic images like *Small storm,* and then there are images of headless children in dark rooms. In both cases, there is a sense of beauty and appealing colors that invite you into the image. Sometimes I find myself wanting to make a more disturbing, unattractive image right after making a very "pretty" image. I need to create a balance for myself in my workflow. In fact, I usually prefer the darker images and sometimes set out to make more unsettling pieces—but they just don't end up that way most of the time. Outside forces tend to support the more positive, upbeat images. The darker images might get people's attention, but they are not images people want to live with.

You mean they don't sell as well? Can you give an example?

> I like *Fragile,* an image that took me quite a long time to make. To me it says something about creativity and the place where ideas originate. When your ideas or your artworks are formed, they're fragile, they come out of your head as these puffy clouds that have to survive on their own. That's why it's called *Fragile.* But other people have been too disturbed by the top of the head being removed, and for whatever reason, this image has not been purchased by too many people.

How well an image will sell is not a factor in making my work—it is just something that happens after the fact. The images have their own, independent, social lives after I finish working on them. Usually once I start working on an image, I keep it in my computer and keep working on it until I am satisfied with it. This might take a week, or (more often) it might be in my computer in one form or another for six months. After a series of stages and changes, when I am ready to part with it and cease working on it, the image goes on to have its own life.

I've been reading about a debate that took place in the late nineteenth century over whether children should read fairy tales, like the Brothers Grimm stories, for example, which can actually be quite terrifying. The pro-fairy tale camp felt that these kinds of stories laid the groundwork for a fertile imagination. Those who opposed them felt that the stories were simply too much for kids to bear, that children should be protected from all that fear and horror as long as possible. I wonder if some people don't have a similar reaction to your darker images and object to them because, on the surface, they seem dark or violent.

> I think children actually have a lot more tolerance for and interest in the dark or frightening stories than adults give them credit for. I am not talking about violence or really gruesome realism. My images are not bloody or really graphic in this sense. Headlessness, for example, serves lots of purposes. It moves the character into the realm of being an Everyman. With the head removed, it's not a specific person and the viewer can project a personality onto the figure. The child in *Strange beast* is actually a friend's grandfather. I loved the image of this smartly dressed boy on his rocking horse, but I didn't want a cute, smiling face, so I removed it. Now he is anyone and everyone's little brother, or grandfather, or nephew.

Another way of thinking about headlessess is that these people have "lost their heads" and therefore lost the ability to deal with reality in a certain way. We are all walking a fine line between things we can cope with and things we can't. I've always been fascinated by stories of seemingly ordinary people crossing over this line into a temporary insanity. The very staid, Victorian characters represented in these old photographs may, in fact, have done all kinds of extraordinary things in their lives and in their dreams. Perhaps they had love affairs with fish, wore rabbit masks, or rode through the woods without their heads.

Many of your images involve animals. Oftentimes, it's an animal-human hybrid, like an animal dressed up in human clothing, or a human with an animal head. Looking at these, I'm reminded of fairy tales and creation stories; there's something very elemental and mythological about them.

> Clearly animals and people have been intertwined in narratives and artwork throughout recorded history. In my work, animals play a number of different roles, sometimes even within the same image. They can be very domesticated and non-threatening, as with the girls who have turned into kittens in *Distracted cats*. Or the animal might disguise or misrepresent the intentions of a person, as with the man wearing a rabbit mask, *Man pretending to be a rabbit*. Then there is the seagull skull in *Just looking*, which is reminiscent of a Venetian mask, which, in turn, references masks worn by physicians during the times of plague in Western Europe. The seagull skull is both mysterious and scary to me, especially as it peers down on a very small person.

Right, birds can signify all kinds of things. Sometimes, they symbolize freedom and release from danger, like in your dreams, perhaps. Other kinds of birds—ravens, crows—can be prophetic, like messengers, here to warn us of something dark on the horizon.

> I like that multiplicity of meanings. It allows there to be space in the images for a variety of interpretations, and for both darkness and humor.

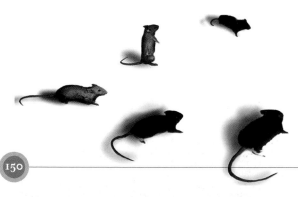

{ Landlocked, 2003. }

{ Water sitters, 2001. }

Pretty busy today, 1999.

{ Small home, 2001. }

{ Bird girls by the sea, 1999. }

commencing *DEC 13th 18 6*, and ending _____

S. H. Callahan

				2d Mo.																			3d Mo.				
M	T	W	T	F		M	T	W	T	F	M	T	W	T	F	M	T	W	T	F	M	T	W	T	F		M	T	W
X	X	X	X	X	18	X	X	X																				

Index